The Man's Guide to Weddings

By John Zakour

and Chuck Schading

The Man's Guide to Weddings
by John Zakour & Chuck Schading
ISBN: 1477564594 / ISBN-13: 9781477564592
©2012 All Rights Reserved

Published by Blue Leaf Publications
"A New Leaf in the Publishing Industry…"
Website: http://www.BlueLeafPub.com
Edited by Dehanna Bailee
Art Credit: A-Elena/ iStockPhoto.com
Art adaptation & interior illustration by Dehanna Bailee

Contents

Prefix

    Introduction   i

1 Pre-Season

    How to propose   1
    Picking the date   3
    Buying the rings   6
    Who pays?   7
    Legal stuff   8
    Should you elope?   9

2 Your Team & Fans

    Invitations   11
    Who to invite   13
    Picking the wedding party   15
    Your wife's shower   18
    Your bachelor party   20
    Her bachelorette party   21

3 The Playbook

    The place   23
    The venue   25
    The cake   27
    The flowers   30
    The dress   32
    The tux   33
    The vows   34
    The photographer   37
    The videographer   39
    The band / music   40
    The meal   42
    The seating   44
    Your bride's gift   45
    Your honeymoon   49
    Wedding planners   51

4 Get Your Game Face On

Cold feet   53
Fighting   54
Stress   57
What to say (a lot)   59
What not to say   60
The in-laws   60
Your parents   63
Your unmarried guy friends 65
Your married guy friends   66
Your ex-girlfriends   68

5 The Big Game

The rehearsal   71
The rehearsal dinner   72
The ceremony   73
The pictures   75
The honeymoon   77
Life-ever-after   77

Appendix

Wedding history and trivia 79
Official definitions   82
Handy wedding definitions 83
Other resources   86

About the Authors   87

To our former fiancées...
Thanks for not saying "I don't."

Prefix

Introduction

First off, it should be pointed out that while weddings are almost always between two people, you—being the guy—are pretty much an innocent bystander for, as you'll soon learn, weddings are first and foremost about the bride. You, the future groom, are just a handy accessory as your future wife, after all, can't become your future wife without you. Still, just because your wedding isn't really about you, it doesn't mean you can't understand, or at least begin to understand, or at least try to begin to understand, what's going on—or, at the very least, try to look like you are trying to begin to understand. Whatever the level of your comprehension, your making an effort will make your future bride happy.

While there are quite a few other books on the market about weddings, most of them (rightly so) are lady centric—as in, they center on the bride. This is fine because, make no bones about it, the bride *is* the star of the wedding; you, however, are just a supporting player. But even supporting players need to know their roles, which is where this book comes in. Written in a "man-friendly" style with lots of small chapters, few if any fancy words, and numerous sports references, *The Man's Guide to Weddings* is designed to help men understand what is going on (and often why). And, while there is a lot of information in this book, even with all of the good stuff, reading it won't qualify you to become a wedding planner, but it can give you a better idea of what to expect. (In other words, after reading this, you should be that much closer to the goal line.)

The actual ceremony will usually take less than an hour; however, the entire wedding process itself is often long and drawn out. To make it easier for guys to comprehend, this book breaks things down into five phases, or stages, as follows:

Pre-Season: *The Basics*

This short little section is designed to make sure you cover the most essential things (like proposing, for one) before you get into the nitty-gritty of the whole wedding planning brouhaha.

The Team & the Fans: *The People*

From the support staff and sideline personnel (bridesmaids and groomsmen), to the ticket-takers (ushers) and fans (you know, all those people who attend your event and eat all your food), this section helps you in getting everyone in place so the big event goes off without a hitch. (It also covers those all-so-important pre-wedding parties, too.)

The Playbook: *Planning the Event*

No matter how long this stage actually is, it will seem much longer because this is the stage where you and your wife-to-be do all the down-and-dirty planning to make the wedding roll as smoothly as possible. You've heard the saying: *The best laid plans of mice and men often get messed up....* That holds true in triplicate for weddings for no matter how much you plan, some 'thing' is going to go wrong—and that's if you're lucky, because in reality a lot of somethings are probably going to go wrong. Somebody is going to forget something. Somebody is not going to show up. Somebody is going to show up who you don't want to show up. Or something else will go wrong. Whatever the issue is, just grin and bear it. Remember, life never goes as planned (and if it did, it would be boring).

Get Your Game Face On: *How to Deal with it All*

From fighting to in-laws, to cold feet or saying the wrong thing, this nifty little section provides you with a selection of tools and tips to help get you all the way through to game day. Hey, we know you love the bride-to-be, but we also know that it's the stresses, doubts, and family matters that can make or break a successful event, so make sure to not miss this part. (It's kind of like your own personal guide on how to keep your opponent—and yourself—in check.)

The Big Game: *The Wedding*

This is the actual ceremony. This event you spent a lot of time planning—unless of course, you're marrying Britney Spears—and this part will fly by. Afterwards you'll be thinking, "Wow, all that planning for something so short." (Just don't say that out loud or the marriage may be short, too.)

And to finish it out, we've also tossed in a short appendix that offers some trivia, definitions, and history. (Which makes for some great neutral topics in case you find yourself in a conversational bind at the rehearsal dinner.)

The Lazy Man's Summary

To make this whole thing a bit less labor intensive, we will have tips and summaries in boxes like this at the end of some sections for you lazy guys. Think of it as just skipping to the score for the basics. (You know— who won, who lost, who hit a home run; how to pick out a cummerbund; what not to say when your bride-to-be starts crying and so forth....)

Pre-Season 1

How to propose

While it's kind of assumed most guys reading this book have already proposed, it is possible some might have received this book as a hint, which is why this part was included. This prefix, or introduction, gives you ideas and methods you can use so your future wife will say "yes" or "sí" or whatever when you ask her to be your wife. Now, if you have already successfully proposed, then consider "prefix" to mean "skip this." But, if your girlfriend gave you this book and you haven't yet proposed to her, then it probably means you are pretty dense because she wants you to propose—and chances are you can say pretty much anything and she will say, "yes."

Yet, if for some reason you're not engaged and your girlfriend didn't give this book, then you may need to work a bit more to get her to accept your proposal. Still, if you're smart and sincere (and actually think a little first), you can make this proposal thing as easy as making a wide-open lay up (note the sports reference, fellas!)—just follow this simple four-step process:

Step 1. Buy an engagement ring.

> This may set you back a bundle, but if you plan to propose, you are going to need one. It's good to consider your bride-to-be when buying the ring. If she is practical, you don't have to go way overboard (just a little overboard is fine). The fact is, even the

most practical woman likes a nice engagement ring. In other words, you should be able to see the diamond with the naked eye. However, if your bride-to-be likes big shiny rings, then buy her a big shiny ring (as in, you should be able to see it with the naked eye from a plane flying overhead). Just remember to keep the receipt in case either you, or the ring, isn't big and shiny enough and she happens to say no.

Step 2. Think about what you are going to say.

You don't have to be Shakespeare or even Stephen King to write a nice proposal—actually, it might be better if you weren't Stephen King—but no matter what you say, you're going to be nervous, so it's best to keep it short and simple. You don't want to give her too much to think about. The KISS technique (Keep It Simple Stupid) is important here and the basic "Will you marry me?" usually gets the job done.

Step 3. Figure out where you want to pop the question.

There are a lot of possibilities: your place, her place, a nice restaurant, a nice park, the Grand Canyon or the International Space Station (if you both happen to be astronauts or have really good connections). Think about where she's happiest and consider proposing there. (Legend tells of one man who actually proposed to his wife in a shoe store.) Take note, though, if you propose in a public place, you run the risk of being rejected in public.

Step 4. Put the previous steps together, get down on one knee, pop the question and then pray.

The answer will either be the thrill of your life (yes, even bigger than the time you scored a game-winning goal) or the beginning of a lifetime of psychotherapy.

Important Note: Whatever you do, do NOT text your proposal to your girlfriend. While, sure, it does mean she won't reject you to your face right then and there, it also greatly reduces the chances of her saying "yes" or "sure" or "why not." Even in today's high-tech age, some things are better done in person.

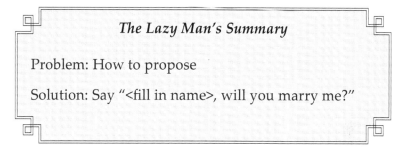

The Lazy Man's Summary

Problem: How to propose

Solution: Say "<fill in name>, will you marry me?"

Picking the date

At this point, if you are still having trouble deciding who to bring (as in marry), drop this book immediately and back away. This section is about having trouble picking a calendar date for your nuptials, not about who to pick to be your wife. (If you knew that, read on.)

Sure, picking a date sounds easy. You and your fiancée just flip through the calendar and choose one day from the available 365. Sounds simple, right? Well, keep reading.

Traditionally, weddings are held on a Saturday or Sunday, and there are only a little over a hundred Saturdays and Sundays in a year to pick from. Odds are also good you will want to get married when you have the best chance of having the least amount of rain (for no bride wants to be soggy), which will further limit your choices. Not to mention all of the holidays, work commitments, football and other sporting events that you need to work around.

Yet, since the wedding is definitely important to your future wife, and probably quite important to you, just make it simple. Pick a Saturday or Sunday during the "nice months" that looks good to both of you then simply say, "This is the day we'll get married." Mark the day on your calendar and keep it free. (In other words, if you must get in a round of golf, do it earlier in the day and stick to nine holes.)

And you'd think that as long as you avoid selecting Super Bowl Sunday as your date, you'd have it made. The thing is, though, while your fiancée may be star of the wedding, and you, her leading man, the wedding is about more than just you two (unless you elope) because your wife will probably want to have a bridal party numbering anywhere from two to twenty; thus, the need for some groomsmen.

Therefore, with that in mind, your fiancée is going to want each of her future bridesmaids to be available because they are all—even the ones she hasn't seen or talked to in years—her "best friends" and she wouldn't begin to think of getting married without them. Heck, there may even be one or two potential groomsmen you actually want there, too, because somebody has to put down a few cold ones with you while your fiancée is busy greeting everyone, after all. So, as a result, it's a good bet that at least one, if not all, of these people, will be busy with something on the original date you picked. If this happens, your options are to either go back to step one and pick a new date or decide you will just have to get through the wedding without everyone you've known since kindergarten in attendance.

The only word of advice here is: No matter what date you pick, odds are somebody is going to be busy that day, and if you change the date, somebody else will be busy on the new one. In reality, you have a better chance of kicking a seventy-yard field goal than finding a date that accommodates everybody, unless you pick a date a couple of years down the road—and even then some of your more anal-retentive friends may already have something planned.

Another potential pitfall to picking a date is that you will need to have many other people beside your friends and family at your wedding. You will also need a place to get married, along with somebody to perform the wedding, a photographer, a caterer, a place to hold the party…. You get the idea. And most likely, your fiancée is going to have pretty set choices for each of these.

Unfortunately, some of these folks won't be available on your original date. Or other people's fiancées are going to want the people your fiancée wants at their weddings, making them either more expensive and/or less available. (For those of you who weren't math majors, neither of these things are good.) Once again, you will be faced with the choice of changing the date or changing your wants. Do whatever's easier. Life is hard enough without making the things that are supposed to be fun hard.

So, overall, your best bet is to remember that as long as you and your bride are there, all will be fine. You may very well have to get married without everyone you—or more likely your wife—wants to be there, whether you—or the wife—like it or not. But you're going to be the easy one; you're just going to be happy somebody is marrying you and will make do with whoever shows up. Your bride-to-be, though, might be convinced that some of her friends are almost as important to the wedding as you. Your job is to convince her that as long as you are there, all will be well. Plus, any friend who won't reschedule their open heart surgery isn't really a friend you want at your wedding anyhow, right?

And, if you need more solid advice, here are a couple of handy hints to help make picking your wedding date as painless as possible:

1. Pick a day that's a few years in the future, like 2070 or 2072. This way you know you can book pretty much everybody and everything.

- or -

2. Pick a date you both like and go with it. Be inflexible about the date, but flexible about everything else. The wedding is pretty much going to be a blur anyway. Just try to convince your fiancée that, as long as you and she are both there, all will be well.

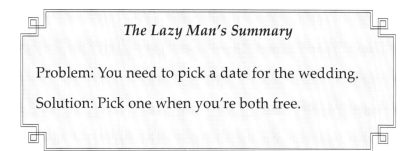

The Lazy Man's Summary

Problem: You need to pick a date for the wedding.

Solution: Pick one when you're both free.

Buying the rings

There was an old commercial that used to say the basic rule of thumb when buying a ring was to: *Use one month's salary.* This is all fine and good, if:

➢ You are wealthy and don't need your salary to pay for things like food and rent.

➢ You own (or work) at a diamond store.

➢ You're not overly bright.

➢ You're hideously ugly and desperate to get married.

Yet, the reality is that if you are an average guy with an average job, you are probably living "pay check to pay check" and really aren't in the position to be giving up a month's salary for a ring. Of course, you can always buy the ring on credit, but then you run the risk of making payments on a ring years after the wedding (or maybe even the marriage) is over.

Your best bet is to convince your future wife she's getting such a great guy she doesn't need an expensive ring. Tell her you can use the money you save on an expensive ring for other things, like a down payment on a house, a nice vacation, or even a new set of his-and-her golf clubs (or just his).

If that doesn't work, it'd be good to start saving now. *(Hey, McDonald's is always hiring....)*

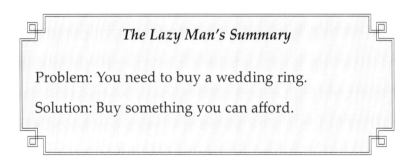

The Lazy Man's Summary

Problem: You need to buy a wedding ring.

Solution: Buy something you can afford.

Who pays?

Back in the olden days it was kind of a tradition for the bride's family to pay for the wedding. This was probably because they had a lot less makeup in the olden days, hence the bride's parents had to do something to encourage some poor sap to marry their daughter. Plus, life expectancy was shorter, so people got married younger, often before they had a chance to save much money.

Today things are different. For one thing, weddings cost more and more (and more), so unless your bride comes from money[1] it would be unreasonable to expect her family to fund the wedding. These days it makes sense for both families to share the expenses—or for the bride and groom to fund the wedding themselves. Sure, it is more costly to you in the short run, but you gain more control. It's a trade-off.

And to help make the trade-off easier, there's a handy chart below. (Charts are cool because you can read them without really paying a lot of attention.) As you look over the options, know that it is probably a good idea to decide who is paying for what well before the bills come rolling in. (It also might not be a bad idea to buy a lottery ticket or two because as they say, *you never know*....)

Deciding Who Pays

Payer	Pros	Cons
Your family	Saves you some bucks.	You'll owe them big time and will hear about it for the rest of your natural born life. You'll also take some ribbing from your friends since your "Mommy and Daddy" paid. *(cont.)*

---

1 See forthcoming, *Man's Guide to Easy Street.*

Your bride's family	Traditional and saves you a bundle.	You'll owe them big time and you'll hear about it for the next several decades.
You and your bride	You'll have complete control— well, as much control as possible, which isn't all that much but is still better than none.	It's going to cost you, so unless you've won the lottery or happen to be rich, it's going to set you back a few house payments.
Some combination	Spreads the expense around.	You owe more people....

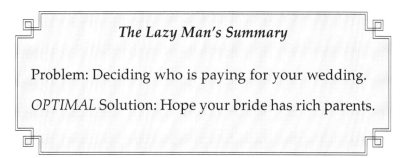

The Lazy Man's Summary

Problem: Deciding who is paying for your wedding.

OPTIMAL Solution: Hope your bride has rich parents.

Legal stuff

Because we live in a modern society, it means to do pretty much anything you are going to have to fill out (and pay for) paperwork. This process creates official documentation and allows the city or state in which you live to make a few fast bucks off of you.

Marriage is no exception because every state (yes, even Arkansas) is going to make you buy and fill out a marriage certificate; there's no way around this.

The costs vary from state to state but since even the most expensive states charge less than a hundred bucks, it shouldn't be a big deal. (If it is, you either shouldn't be getting married or you should be looking for somebody a lot richer to marry.)

Some states will require that both you and your fiancée take blood tests. No, this isn't to make sure neither of you is an alien. It's to see if either of you might have a sexuality transmitted disease, which, when you think about it, is a good thing. So, if you live in a state that requires such a test, it's no big deal. You're a man. You should be able to take a little prick. (And, if you can't take a little prick, then you seriously need to consider if you are hardy enough for marriage to begin with.)

Others may also require "waiting periods" of a couple of days from when the license is filed to when you can actually marry. This is designed to give your fiancée some time to come to her senses. (Apparently some states consider marriage as dangerous as guns. Texas, however, actually considers guns to be safer than marriage.)

To find out what the requirements are in your state, do a Web search — or better yet, pay a visit to your city hall or county clerk's office and ask them what the requirements are. After all, since your hard-earned tax dollars are paying these people's salaries, you might as well put them to work a bit.

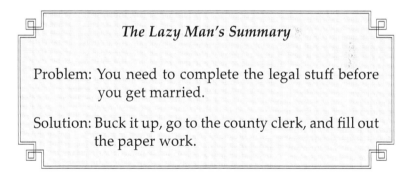

The Lazy Man's Summary

Problem: You need to complete the legal stuff before you get married.

Solution: Buck it up, go to the county clerk, and fill out the paper work.

Should you elope?

At some point in the wedding process things are going to become such a pain that you and your bride will suddenly look at each other and say, "Should we elope?"

Well, the answer is easy: Yes, you should elope. Why? Well, for one, it will save you a lot of headaches. And then afterwards, once you are married, you can have a big party.

Still, you probably won't elope because:

1. Your bride has always wanted a proper wedding.

2. You don't want to upset your parents.

3. You look fabulous in a tux.

However, on the off chance you might actually consider it, there are a few things you may want to think about first:

THE PROS OF ELOPING

➢ It's faster. You don't even have to set a date.

➢ It's cheaper. You don't have to pay for a bunch of third-cousins-once-removed to come to your wedding.

➢ It's a lot less hassle. You don't have to worry about forgetting to invite your rich-but-crazy uncle because you won't be inviting anybody else either.

THE CONS OF ELOPING

➢ You will piss off your mother and your fiancée's mother. (Though some of you may think of this as a pro. Actually, if your fiancée's family is paying, chances are her dad won't be too upset with you.)

➢ You'll lose out on a boatload of presents.

All in all, the final decision will be up to your fiancée and you.

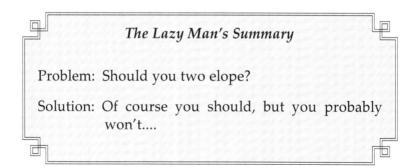

The Lazy Man's Summary

Problem: Should you two elope?

Solution: Of course you should, but you probably won't....

Your Team & Fans   2

Invitations

You're a guy. If it was up to you, you'd simply pick up the phone and call all your friends and say, "I'm getting married, why don't you come? There'll be beer! Bring more."

Your future wife, of course, isn't going to go for this. It's funny— most of time you'll find your wife will be much more practical than you. She'll point out things like how you don't really need a 55-inch, HD Plasma TV while you're still sitting on the floor because you don't have enough money for a couch—but when it comes to invitations, something you could do just as easily with a mass text or a strategically placed Facebook post, she won't hear of it. She'll say it's not proper and "Sure, we can afford the gold-plated cards with raised platinum print!" And no matter what you say, she will insist you need to send formal invitations.

At first you'll think, "How bad can it be?" After all, how many ways can you say, *"Come to our wedding*?" Oh, won't you be surprised. One day your future wife will bring you at least one book that is thicker than any two huge dictionaries you've ever seen (and we're talking unabridged). This book will be filled with hundreds, if not thousands, of possible invitations. They all say basically the same things, *"Come to our wedding," "This is the date," "This is the place,"* but they say it in many, many, many different fonts, styles, faces, colors, and a bunch of other things you don't really care that much about.

Of course you'll also be surprised how much your fiancée cares about them. You'll find she not only wants you to "help" pick out the invitations themselves, but the envelopes and response cards and response card envelopes as well. All in all, this can be far more complicated than putting together a carburetor with only one good hand, and not nearly as fun.

Your strategy here is to look through the cards and related items and do your best to pretend to care. It helps to use phrases such as:

➢ "This one's nice!"

➢ "You have much better taste than I do!"

➢ "Hmm, yes, I see what you mean."

➢ "Yes, the blue in that flower matches your eyes."

➢ "Wow, this is much more fun than watching the game."

When you will be thinking things like:

➢ "I can't believe I'm doing this!"

➢ "I can't believe these things cost that much! What are they lined with, melted down Stanley Cup trophies?"

➢ "Where is the mother-in-law when I need her?"

➢ "Is the game on yet?"

The bottom line is, while your fiancée says she wants your feedback and input, what she really wants is for you to agree with her.

The rock bottom line is they are *freaking cards*, silly pieces of paper, and you don't give a horse's hoot about them. Your most important concern is to try to steer your bride-to-be away from invitations that cost more than your first car did.

Of course, if she really wants to go with the expensive ones, your only hope could be to pretend to like them so much, she'll become convinced there must be something wrong with them.

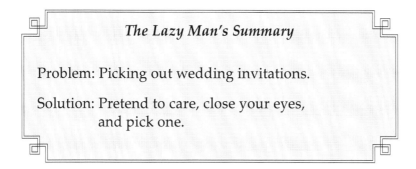

The Lazy Man's Summary

Problem: Picking out wedding invitations.

Solution: Pretend to care, close your eyes,
           and pick one.

Who to invite

You may think this will be easy. After all, how many really good friends do you have? Not a lot probably. So, in essence, all you really need to do is to make a list of your friends, and your wife's friends, and combine them. Then you'll need to talk for a bit to decide who to invite, and who not to invite. Then you will just need to send invites to all the people on this list. Easy, right?

In theory. However, what is often easy in theory usually isn't in execution, and sending invites to your get-together often becomes a complicated exercise in dynamic human relations, where you will soon learn things like:

➢ "Uncle Charlie won't come if Aunt Clare is there."

➢ "Uncle Charlie won't come unless Uncle Bob is there."

➢ "Uncle Charlie won't come if there's not an open bar."

➢ "Last wedding, Uncle Charlie and Aunt Mary had a knock-down, drag-out fight. Neither will come if the other is there."

➢ "My mom says we have to invite Betsy and Louie, our third-cousins-once-removed, because even though we don't know what third-cousins-once-removed actually are, their parents invited us to their fortieth anniversary party."

And take note, the phrase "My mom says" is something you will likely be hearing a lot. Making out the invitations will probably be the first time you realize you'll soon have a mother-in-law. A few seconds later you will learn that most mothers-in-law feel it is their God-given right to make your life harder. (After all, their daughter drove them crazy from the time they turned ten to however old they are now. So, now they are going to get revenge by taking it out on you—starting with the guest list you thought would be easy to compile.)

Mothers-in-law probably don't mean to do this, because contrary to most fairy tales (and old husband's tales), not all of them are pure evil. So, where does this bad rap come from? A subconscious, passive-aggressive need to take revenge out on somebody probably, but they can't take it out on their daughter—after all, she will be the one to bear the grandkids—so they will instead vent on you.

But, don't just think it's only going to be coming from your fiancée's side because your mom is also going to have an opinion. And when it comes to who gets an invite, your future wife will probably rank your mom's opinion slightly ahead of yours, figuring your mom is a woman so she knows more than you do about this type of stuff. However, your future wife will also figure your mom is not genetically related to her, so she doesn't know all that much. (If your future wife and mom are related, then you're going to have problems that go way beyond the scope of this book.[2])

And while they may say the best defense is a good offense, in this situation the best offense is most likely a good defense. Simply say, "Yes, I agree," a lot. If you are agreeing with your fiancée, it might also help to add a "dear" to that sentence.

Also, when it comes to the guest list, you're not going to remember most of the people who are there anyhow. If the truth be told, probably less than three percent of men who have been married more than five years can identify more than two percent of the people in their wedding photos. So, don't sweat it. Smile and play nice.

Plus, the nice thing about agreeing most of the time is that it gives you a little leeway for putting the kibosh on somebody you find

---

2 See forthcoming *The Redneck's Guide to Weddings* for help.

really egregious or annoying (i.e.: your old gym teacher, your great aunt with the handlebar mustache who loves explosives, or perhaps even one of your bride's girlfriends who also happens to be your ex-girlfriend).

So, when you do say, "Let's think about skipping them to save money," your wife will be more likely to agree, since you've agreed with ninety-nine percent of her other decisions. She has to give you something. If you have to, you can even remind her of how "Marriage is about give and take...." (Women love those types of things.)

Overall, as long you make sure to invite your two or three best buddies, you'll be fine, since this will give you somebody to hang out with while your wife is greeting the hordes of people she and her mom (and maybe your mom) invited who you don't know to begin with.

 Note: Don't say, "Yes, dear," to your mother-in-law or mother. One is just plain wrong, and the other is just plain creepy.

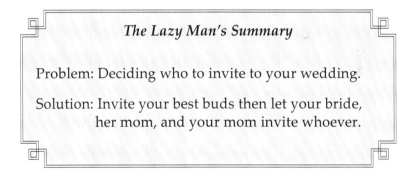

The Lazy Man's Summary

Problem: Deciding who to invite to your wedding.

Solution: Invite your best buds then let your bride, her mom, and your mom invite whoever.

Picking the wedding party

Your wedding party will consist of two to (way) more than two people. You will have a best man and your wife will have a maid or matron of honor. (The maid or matron of honor are really the exact same thing except for one thing: One of them is married. Although, if you really want to know, it's the matron that's already hitched.)

The wedding party is important because these are the people who will take part in the wedding with you. The best man and maid/

matron of honor have the responsibility of being official witnesses to your wedding. Without them, your marriage wouldn't be legal, and the last thing you want is to have an illegal wedding.

The remaining members of the wedding party are somewhat like figureheads; kind of like the Queen of England—as in, they get all dressed up, but wield no real power.

Your other groomsmen have the job of walking people down the aisle and leading them to their seats. This really isn't that challenging of a job. In fact, trained chimps could probably do it just as well as your buds, if not better. Heck, your wedding would proceed just fine without them considering the majority of your guests are probably quite able to find a seat and sit on their butts without assistance.

The bridesmaids have even less to do. Their job is basically to stand around and try to look pretty in ridiculous looking dresses. (The theory is bridesmaids' dresses are designed to be ridiculous looking in order to help make the bride herself look even better.)

You, though—being a guy—probably don't have a lot of close friends, so it makes it easier to pick who you want to have in your wedding party because you already know who your good buddies are. They are the ones who stood by you through thick and thin. The ones who made you drink until you barfed. The ones who don't correct you when you add a few points to your bowling average, or look the other way when you use your "foot wedge" every once in a while on the golf course. Those are the ones you want in your wedding.

However, chances are good your fiancée will want to have more bridesmaids than you have groomsmen. So, naturally, she will agonize over who to pick. Keep in mind, Supreme Court justices have been selected with less effort than your fiancée will put into to picking her bridesmaids, as she frets over who to choose, based on such weird factors as:

> ➢ I was in her wedding.

> ➢ We were sorority sisters.

> ➢ Her parents and my parents are best friends.

- ➢ She's one of my ten or twenty closest friends.
- ➢ We talked once in high school.
- ➢ We talked once in college.
- ➢ It would mean a lot to her.
- ➢ She introduced me to you.
- ➢ I owe her money.
- ➢ She owes me money.
- ➢ She gave me a kidney.
- ➢ She's my friend on Facebook.
- ➢ I stole you from her.

At this point, you're probably thinking, "So, how does this affect me? I already have my groomsmen!" Well, the thing is, traditionally, you will be expected to have just as many groomsmen as your bride has bridesmaids—which leaves you with two strategies:

1. Convince your fiancée traditions suck and it's cool to have an unbalanced wedding party.

2. Pick a bunch of other guys you're not close to (or, for that matter, ones you just grabbed off the street, bar, or playing field) and roll with it.

There is one decision you may actually think about a bit about, which is who to pick for your best man. But, you really shouldn't sweat it. Most straight guys don't mind one way or another if they are in a wedding or not. Sure, it's an honor, but it's not like they just won the Heisman trophy or anything. As long as they get to go, drink beer, bust your chops, and hit on cute chicks, your friends will be happy. In fact, most guys would probably prefer not to be in the wedding party (unless your wife has a few hot bridesmaids). So, when it comes down to it, you may just end up picking your best man by simply deciding which of your friends (or relatives) would be the least pissed if you did (or didn't) pick them.

Note: Fun—but slightly evil—idea: To have a little fun with your unmarried groomsmen, convince your wife to have one, and only one, really hot-looking, unattached bridesmaid. You'll get to experience the joy of watching your friends fight over this woman's attention (and other things) throughout your blessed day.

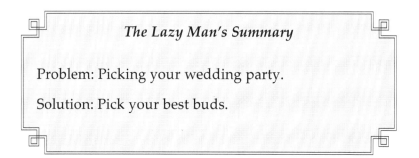

The Lazy Man's Summary

Problem: Picking your wedding party.

Solution: Pick your best buds.

Your wife's shower

(Guys, don't get all excited; this just means "your wife's party.")

It's inevitable that your wife's friends are going to want to throw her a shower. This way they can celebrate her getting married and, at the same time, console her that she's getting married to you.

Showers are mostly harmless. Other women shower your wife with gifts and wisdom about what married life will be like, usually over a light meal. It's bonding time for them and free time for you. At least it used to be.... Back in the olden days (until around 1990), showers were decidedly "ladies only," which was cool. The guy (you) could just hang out and do whatever—catch the game, belch, scratch, spend some quality time with his buds, play poker, or just hang.

Modern times, however, have thrown us a wicked curve ball. Not only do we have good things like HDTV, pointless-but-addictive cell phone apps, a multitude of cable channels and more kinds of beer, we also have things like Lifetime Network and "coed bridal showers."

That's right, "coed bridal showers." Which means, if your wife's friends do decide to give her a coed shower, not only will you lose a day to yourself, you will also be forced to sit around and smile nice while you watch your wife open presents. Meanwhile, her friends will share their vast knowledge with both of you—mostly consisting of what jerks men are and how they don't always obey. It's not quite castration, but at times it might as well be (especially since it's likely that there won't even be beer).

So, what you'll need to do is try to convince your fiancée's friends or family (or whoever is throwing her the shower) that it will be much more fun for all of them if they keep it void of men. Remind them of things like:

➢ Men smell funny.

➢ Men burp a lot.

➢ Quiche and men aren't a good mix. (See above options.)

➢ They'd have a lot more fun without men.

➢ They would feel less self-conscious and restricted talking about men without any actual men being around.

➢ It will cost a lot more if they invite you and other men, since men eat like pigs.

If the above strategies fail and for some unfathomable reason they still decide to have a coed shower, your options are limited. You can fake being sick, but this is a drastic move you may want to save for later in your married life to help you get out of something really heinous, like going to the opera or a trip to your in-laws.

The next option is to accept there is nothing you can do and simply go to the shower. Put on your best fake smile, nod your head, and plan to say "that's lovely" a lot. Just keep your fingers crossed that the place has a TV so you and can sneak off to catch the game.

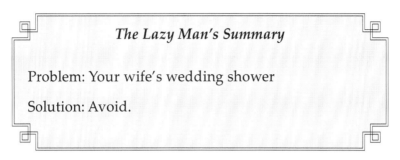

The Lazy Man's Summary

Problem: Your wife's wedding shower

Solution: Avoid.

Your bachelor party

You're a guy. You know what a bachelor party is. This is where your friends throw themselves a party and pretend it's about you. There will be food and lots to drink. Your friends may also have one or more women there who just can't seem to keep their shirts on, and it's quite possible your future wife won't approve. Which means, you may be thinking, "Well, after this, I will be with one woman forever...so, what can it hurt? After all, I'm not married yet, right?"

Wrong. Remember, there is one golden rule at any bachelor party these days:

EVERYBODY HAS CAMERA PHONES SO DON'T DO ANYTHING STUPID THAT CAN COME BACK TO HAUNT YOU. YOU <u>DO NOT</u> WANT TO SEE YOURSELF ON YOUTUBE IN THE MORNING!!

And for those of you still struggling with this concept, it means:

KEEP YOUR PANTS ON AND THE VIDEO CAMERA OFF!!

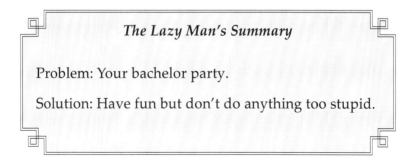

The Lazy Man's Summary

Problem: Your bachelor party.

Solution: Have fun but don't do anything too stupid.

Her bachelorette party

Acting stupid at bachelor parties used to be solely the domain of men, but that's all changed, thanks to cultural adjustments and TV shows like "Jersey Shore" and "Desperate Housewives." This shift has made women realize that they are sexual beings too with the right to make fools of themselves before they become committed to just one man (with, hopefully, that one man being you).

But with that in mind, you should probably make a note to be extra nice to your fiancée in the days leading up to the party. If for nothing else, just to help remind her about what a great guy you are.

If it helps, you can also use handy phrases like:

> "Boy, I sure love you."

> "I'm so lucky to be getting married to you."

> "I hear most male strippers are gay...."

And while you may feel a tinge of fear as she loads into the limo with her gal pals, you can take comfort in the fact that women usually have more common sense than men. So, the chances are quite good your fiancée will just have a bit of fun, and maybe let loose a bit at the party, but in the end she'll realize you are the only guy for her (even if the other women don't put money in your "man thong").

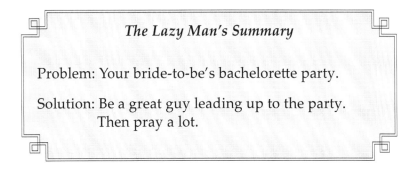

The Lazy Man's Summary

Problem: Your bride-to-be's bachelorette party.

Solution: Be a great guy leading up to the party.
Then pray a lot.

The Playbook   3

The place

Tradition says, "Couples are to get married in the bride's hometown. "

Well, this is all nice and quaint, but with today's mobile society a lot of brides aren't really sure what to call their hometown. They may have been born in one town, raised in another, and then maybe moved to another town or two, so home probably happens to be wherever they happen to be at the time.

The best thing to do is to talk to your fiancée and find out where she wants to get married. If she has a set idea, like her hometown or the current town in which she is living, then it's settled because this is where the tradition of getting married in the bride's hometown comes in handy.

That's the role of tradition plays; it allows us to accept some things without thinking. (You have enough to worry about; the less thinking you need to do the better.)

However, if your fiancée is not sure where she wants to get married, then she might ask you for input. If it happens, you need to be ready to do your part and make some suggestions.

If this is the case, it might help to review the handy reference chart on the next page to get an idea of your options:

Tips for Picking the Place

The Place	Pros	Cons
The town you both live in.	Cheaper for you and maybe your friends since they won't need to find a place to stay.	Might be a bit boring.
Niagara Falls	A great place to honeymoon is also a really nice place to get married.	If traveling, could get expensive. Kind of cliché.
Vegas	Probably the home of more unplanned weddings than any other city but can be a cool place to get married, even when you do plan ahead. Lots of stars get married two or three (or more) times here.	Could be expensive, especially if you like roulette.
Hawaii	Hey, it's Hawaii; 'nuff said...	The expense and the fact that you may not want to go back to the mainland.
Costa Rica	A hot wedding place due to the weather and the beaches are wonderful. They even have a place where you can get married in the tree tops. (We're not making this up.)	Could be expensive: air travel, passports. Everybody around you will be speaking Spanish, which could be a problem if you don't.

(cont...)

Boise	Think of the fun you can have telling people, "Yep, we got married in Boise."	Not really known as a wedding site, but we've decided to try to make it one because we like typing Boise.

The Lazy Man's Summary

Problem: Picking a place to get married.

Solution: If in doubt, get married in the same town you plan to call home. It just makes sense.

The venue

Your fiancée has been planning for this moment since her first Barbie doll eloped with Ken behind the living room sofa, and as a result she probably has a solid opinion on this. And, as before, there are a lot more choices than you would think. Again, your job is to be supportive and toss out suggestions, mainly because it's good to show your wife and her mother (and your mother) that you do have an opinion and like to be useful. Heck, you just want to get married and start having guilt-free sex. You'll do whatever to make it so. You'd do it in a bar if you could (if you could get your fiancée to agree, that is). Just to make it easy, we're including another chart that lists a few of the pros and cons of possible wedding venues.

Tips for Picking the Venue

Place	Pros	Cons
Your home, her home, a friend's home	Probably the least expensive choice, kind of quaint.	Do you really want a bunch of your friends wandering around your house?
		(cont...)

Church	Traditional, lots of seats, usually not too expensive.	Traditional. Won't work if you or your bride are atheists or agnostics. Also, if you go to different churches, could lead to a dispute.
Party House *(Reception Hall)*	You're going to have the party there, so why not get married there; less travel.	Not as personal as other choices. Might be other weddings going on at the same time.
Country Club	Nice atmosphere, plus you can get in nine holes while the bride is having her pictures taken (but don't actually try this or you may have the shortest wedding in history).	Expensive, plus your bride probably won't let you get in a quick nine holes.
City Hall	A nice choice for quick simple weddings especially if you're not very religious.	Probably can't have the party there.
The lake or a park	Nice choice for nature types; usually not all that costly.	Trouble if it rains and could draw complaints from non-nature-loving types.

Note: You could have the ceremony in one spot and the reception in another.

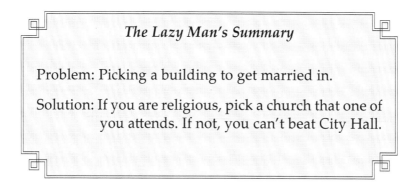

The Lazy Man's Summary

Problem: Picking a building to get married in.

Solution: If you are religious, pick a church that one of
you attends. If not, you can't beat City Hall.

The cake

Okay, we know. You've been dealing with (and eating) cake for a long time—probably since your first birthday, when you gleefully threw your face into your birthday cake. Well, get ready. Your wedding cake will be like no cake you've ever experienced before.

Sure, eventually your new bride is going to follow tradition and shove a piece into your mouth, which you will then follow by shoving a piece into her mouth. This is all great fun, quite reminiscent of your first birthday, but the road to this fun is going to be lined with lots of decisions. And your fiancée certainly will not take your opinions about the cake as law, but she'll at least listen to what you have to say. After all, eating cake is something you probably excel at; it's a skill for which you have demonstrated your proficiency with in front of her on many occasions.

First off, you'll have to decide who will bake the cake. This can be quite fun (and even more fattening) as you get to go from bakery to bakery sampling their wares (as in, eating lots of cake). Plus, to make things even more fun, your future bride will probably be dieting so she can fit into her wedding dress, therefore, you will get to do most (or at least more) of the sampling.

Although, while on your cake-seeking adventure, you're again going to be amazed at the seemingly endless list of possible varieties and variables you will have to choose from, which may include, and certainly aren't limited to:

Flavor

> Yes, you may want chocolate, but tradition tends to lean towards vanilla, because it's "pure" like your bride. (Stop laughing.) So, there's a good chance you won't get chocolate. But you will be amazed at the number of vanilla flavors there are. And while you may think they all taste the same, and they very well might, don't ever say this out loud, especially in front of the "cake chef," or you are likely to get a spatula put some place you certainly don't want a spatula put.

Filling

> This runs the gamut from white to creamy white to all sorts of fruits and probably even some vegetable fillings. You're a guy, you probably don't care, but your fiancée might. To simplify, think of it as "art" — as in, you might not quite understand it, but you know what you like.

Frosting

> Once again, you will be faced with way more choices than you would have thought possible, especially since your fiancée probably won't let you pick chocolate. (If she does, then you are a lucky man who probably doesn't deserve her.) Just know going in that you'll probably end up picking "some shade of white or off white."

Layers

> Wedding cakes need layers. Lots of them. It's just how they are. The baker will quite likely have an estimate of how many layers of cake you will need to feed the number of guests you will have at your wedding. And, no, the calculation isn't nearly as complicated as figuring out the amount of fuel a rocket will need

to escape Earth's atmosphere. It just seems that way. Just nod your head and agree with whatever the "cake chef" says. (Remember the spatula.)

Decorations

You're probably familiar with how wedding cakes have fake little brides and grooms on top of them. This is to remind the folks who have come to your wedding that, yes, it is a wedding they are attending. (Apparently, seeing you and your bride dressed up isn't enough for some people; they need the actual figurines on the wedding cakes, as well.) And there are probably more combinations of fake brides and grooms to put on your cake than actual brides and grooms in the world. Just don't sweat it and you'll be fine. In the big picture, nobody is going to remember what the bride and groom on the cake looked like (unless you can convince your bride-to-be to use a naked bride and groom, but odds are pretty slim you'll be able to pull it off).

 Note: Some people who have way too much money actually have their fake bride and groom cake ornaments made to look like them which, when you think about it, is kind of creepy.

The bottom line is, despite all the fuss and muss, it is still just a cake. It's going to be a blur when your wife shoves it into your mouth and nose anyhow. Remember, chew, swallow, then shove some (lovingly) down your wife's throat and you'll be fine. Whatever choices you make will be tasty and expensive. Your goal is to hope you can keep the cost of the cake (as with most other wedding expenditures) to around what you probably paid for your first car.

 Hint: If her mother likes to bake, let her make the cake. Not only will it save some valuable money but it will make your future mother-in-law happy. A happy mother in-law means you have a happy bride and a happy bride means a happier, less hassled, you.

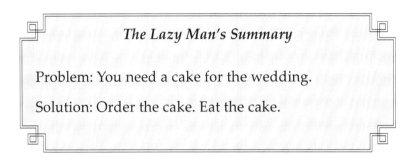

The Lazy Man's Summary

Problem: You need a cake for the wedding.

Solution: Order the cake. Eat the cake.

The flowers

Okay, you're a guy, the only thing you probably care about when it comes to flowers is, "How much are they going to cost?" However, you can't say this to your future wife because she will think you are an "insensitive slug" and you really don't want her finding that out until you are married for at least a month.

Your wife and her flower consultant (yes, there are such things) will tell you that you need flowers all over the place. Of course, you know your wife needs to carry a bouquet of flowers down the aisle. These flowers are fun for eventually your wife will toss them in the air and you'll get to watch her single friends roll around on the floor and grapple for them. Hey, you'll be married by then, but not dead…a good cat fight is a good cat fight. (You may even want to think about a weapons check at the door because these flower fights can sometimes get downright ugly.)

What you may not have known, and probably never thought of, is that you will (according to the consultant) also need flowers on the tables, at the wedding site, and lots of other places you never would have imagined flowers would be needed, seeing you are not a flower consultant. And as you are probably aware, there are a lot of types of flowers in the world, but you'll be surprised to learn there are way (WAY!) more types of flowers than you thought possible. (Unless, of course, you are a flower consultant.)

Because of all the choices, you are probably going to be thinking: *"Hey they're just flowers. They look okay, but they're going to die within days, if not hours. Let's not spend our first few months mortgage on them."*

Yet, once again, you have to make sure you never, ever even think of saying this out loud. Otherwise, you run the risk of your bride figuring out that you are an insensitive lout way sooner than you want her to. (Not to mention how it can make the flower consultant all pissy and we all know how ugly it can get when you piss off a flower consultant.)

In any case, your best bet is to nod your head and say things like:

- ➤ "Yes, those are nice."

- ➤ "Hmmm, I may be all man, but I still find these ones kind of pretty."

- ➤ "These have a nice color."

- ➤ "These smell nice."

- ➤ "Hey, those remind me of the new Lakers uniforms!"

And while you are saying all that, make sure you also check out the prices because your goal is to get the cheapest flowers possible. Why? Well, for one, they just are freaking flowers, after all. You don't need to spend a year's rent on something that will die in a day.

So, after the consultant tells you the price, if you think they are too expensive, which you will, just start to sniffle and sneeze a lot. Then say, "Jeez, honey, I must be allergic to these. I'd hate to ruin the wedding with my sneezing," because chances are your bride won't want you sneezing throughout the wedding, much less getting her dress that she will never wear again dirty.

And, remember, even if somebody else is paying for the flowers, it can still come back to bite you.

Honestly, you wouldn't want your father-in-law to turn you down for a little loan five years down the road because he's still paying for those special thornless, long-stem, golden roses you just had to have imported from Costa Rica for your wedding, now would you?

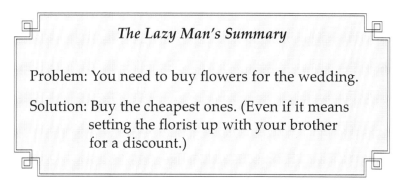

The Lazy Man's Summary

Problem: You need to buy flowers for the wedding.

Solution: Buy the cheapest ones. (Even if it means setting the florist up with your brother for a discount.)

The dress

If she's like most brides, you're going to find out very quickly how you will have very little influence on the dress decision. In fact, absolutely none. For one thing, you are guy. You know nothing about dresses.[3] For another, tradition says you're not supposed to even see the dress until your bride walks down the aisle wearing it.

Regardless, your fiancée will still want feedback, so even though you can't see the actual dress, you can and will see pictures of the dress, along with many, many, many other dresses. You may be aware there are magazines, web sites and catalogs devoted to wedding dresses, but you have no idea the number of magazines, web sites and catalogs devoted to wedding dresses.

And it's amazing the amount of thought and money[4] that will be put into something your wife-to-be will only wear once; however, you probably shouldn't think about it—and you definitely shouldn't mention it out loud.

If you're lucky, your fiancée may want to follow family tradition and wear her mom's wedding dress down the aisle. If so, this could save you enough money to extend your honeymoon a week or maybe two. Chances are, though, you're not going to be that lucky.

So, the response strategies for the bridal dress are easy:

---

3 If you do happen to know a lot about dresses, then you should probably put down this book and wait for *The Girly Man's Guide to Weddings*.

4 If you were to fund a study, it would probably show that Everest could be climbed with less expense and effort than what is involved with dress shopping.

1. Hope your fiancée decides on one that costs less than your first and second cars combined, or at least that the shoes she picks out won't cost more than a nice motorcycle.

2. Be proactive; it's risky but potentially rewarding. Compliment your wife's taste in dresses then give subtle hints how you two aren't made of money and that you two have lots of other things to buy to start your lives together. (Good luck with this one.)

 Note: When in doubt always say, "You look great in everything you wear." This will apply throughout your married life.

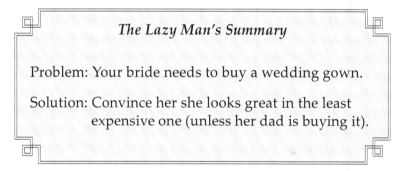

The Lazy Man's Summary

Problem: Your bride needs to buy a wedding gown.

Solution: Convince her she looks great in the least expensive one (unless her dad is buying it).

The tux

While you will spend much time and money on your fiancée's gown, the reverse holds true for your tux. For some reason, it's okay for the groom to simply rent their get-up, which just goes to prove you're not much more than another accessory.

Still, your fiancée will want to make sure you are a snappy-looking accessory. And since you are a guy, you obviously wouldn't know snappy-looking if it walked up, slapped you silly, then kicked you in the crotch. Therefore, your fiancée will probably insist on coming with you to the rental shop.

All in all, the process will be mostly harmless. You'll go to the store and look at more tuxedos than you probably thought (or cared) existed, but no matter how long it takes, you will need to find one you like—and more importantly, one that your fiancée approves of.

A tailor will then tailor the tux to fit you. This is also painless, although it might seem as if the tailor is having way too much fun taking your measurements. (But, hey, tailors probably lead pretty boring lives and need to get their kicks anyway they can. You probably shouldn't make too much of a fuss about it or the tailor might leave in a pin in a very inappropriate and painful spot.) However, in case your wife doesn't come with you to the rental shop, here are a few things to definitely avoid:

➢ Pastels

➢ Ruffles

➢ Plaids

➢ Stars and stripes

➢ Camouflage

➢ Sports team and/or NASCAR-style logos

➢ Top hats and canes (unless she requests it)

➢ Shorts

➢ Sneakers or flip flops

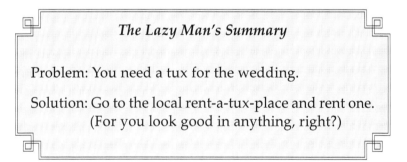

The Lazy Man's Summary

Problem: You need a tux for the wedding.

Solution: Go to the local rent-a-tux-place and rent one. (For you look good in anything, right?)

The vows

Not all couples write their own vows, but it is becoming more and more common. So, while you may not have to write your own vows, it's best to be prepared—but don't worry, it's not that hard. You don't have to be William Shakespeare (he was a famous writer who wrote even more than Stephen King) to write a vow that will wow your bride. For motivation, remember a wowed bride will be happy a bride (and that should at least get you some good sex).

First off, there are a few things you should avoid:

> *Don't use a lot of sports metaphors.* For instance, while "You mean more to me than a hole in one" is certainly an interesting metaphor, it's not a good wedding vow metaphor unless you happen to be marrying a pro golfer.

> *Don't compare your bride to beer.* Wine, maybe; but beer and most other alcoholic beverages, including margaritas and fuzzy navels, should be avoided. It's just not a good idea unless your bride happens to be a lush or a member of the Miller family (in which case, congratulations are in order).

> *Don't compare your bride to past girlfriends.* This just won't work, except on the off chance your bride is a closet lesbian. But that comes with its own set of issues.[5]

> *Don't compare her to, or even mention, your favorite TV show*—unless it happens to be her favorite show and/ or that's how you met. For example, many couples have met over *Star Trek* (strange, but true), so in that case, "I love you more than Kirk loves Spock," for example, would be entirely appropriate.

> *Never even think of mentioning "Jersey Shore."* Heck, you shouldn't think of this even if you're Pauly D.

> *Avoid clichés like: "My life started the moment I met you." "You light up my life." "The early bird catches the worm." "It's always darkest before the dawn." "It's not over until it's over."* Even though these clichés may be perfectly true, your bride is going to expect original thoughts. (Yep, brides can be demanding.)

---

5 See forthcoming, *Man's Guide to Restoring Your Shattered Ego.*

Now, here are some tips to help you write good vows:

➢ *Think about flowers.* I know you're a guy and you don't usually think of flowers, but women like flowers. This is a mental exercise that will put you in the right frame of mind to write something your bride will like. You can even compare her to a beautiful flower as long as you can do it without being cliché.

➢ *List your bride's good traits*—and mention them.

 Note: However, if you consider one of her good traits to be her "huge jiggly breasts," you probably shouldn't mention it.

➢ *Be modest.* Let her know how lucky you feel that a chump like you landed a lady like her.

➢ *Remind her she's beautiful.* Women might say they don't need to hear this, but they do.

➢ *Mention how much you love her*—as many times as you can without being sappy.

➢ *Keep each vow to around eighteen seconds.*[6]

When speaking your vows, say them clearly. You will also gain a lot of brownie points if you can get your eyes to water some. (If you need help doing this, and you will because you're a guy, just think about the great set of golf clubs you could have bought with the money spent on the bridal gown.)

 Note: After you write your vows, don't forget to bring them to the wedding ceremony (just in case you can't recall them when you're at the altar). A good tip is to give a copy to your future father- or mother-in-law. It's their little girl you're marrying; they definitely won't let you forget them.

---

6 Eighteen seconds worth of verbal information is about the maximum amount humans can keep in their short-term memory.

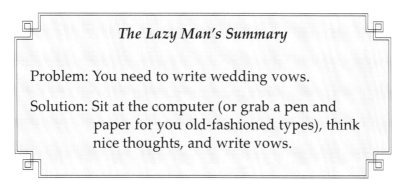

The Lazy Man's Summary

Problem: You need to write wedding vows.

Solution: Sit at the computer (or grab a pen and
paper for you old-fashioned types), think
nice thoughts, and write vows.

The photographer

First off, hopefully, you have a friend who is a photographer, or at least handy with a camera. If not, then now would be a good time to befriend a photographer. Sure, most photographers might be a bit "different," but for what they charge to do a wedding, it's worth your time to hang out with one for a while.

If you can't (or won't) befriend a photographer, then you're going to have to hire one. Photographers can be difficult to work with, so your fiancée may assign this duty to you. (Plus, for some reason, photography is often thought of as a "man thing," like spitting and leaving the seat up. Probably goes back to when old-time cameras were big and bulky and difficult to drag around.)

We won't go into the cost factor because pricing varies; yet, no matter where you live, you will pay far more than you would like to pay. (And while you wouldn't think it's all that hard to just 'point and click,' apparently, it's a lot trickier—or at least a lot more expensive—than one originally thought.)

The process of selecting one is also pretty boring. You two will go from photographer to photographer and each will show you their "book" of other weddings they shot. (FYI: These people will all look alike, but nothing like you.)

The photographers will also describe their options; hence, as you pretend to attentively listen, remember how hiring a photographer is a lot like buying a new car, except the photographer will cost a bit less and you only have them for a day.

Note: A cheap option is to leave disposable cameras on the tables at your reception and let the guests take pictures. Collect the cameras at the end of the event and develop the pictures. The greatest downside to this is that you might end up with a photo album full of cut-off heads...or worse.

Another Note: A cheaper option is to just ask everybody to use their cell phone cameras to take pictures and email them to you.

While there are a lot of good wedding photographers out there (face it, it's not brain surgery—heck, it's not even hemorrhoid surgery) there are still a lot of sham artists, so be careful when choosing one for your wedding.

Here are a few hints that may indicate whether a photographer is any good (or not):

> If their office is their car, avoid.

> If they don't want to do pictures in color because it's "just a fad," avoid.

> If they offer to use Photoshop to enhance your wife's assets, probably should avoid.

> If they offer to take nude shots of your wife, avoid.

> If they offer to show you nudes of your wife, punch in the nose, then avoid.

> If they offer to take nudes of you, really avoid. (Unless of course they are willing to give you a really good price on the wedding pictures.)

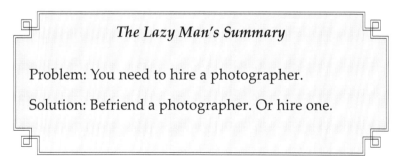

The Lazy Man's Summary

Problem: You need to hire a photographer.

Solution: Befriend a photographer. Or hire one.

The videographer

Our parents only had to worry about photographers at their wedding; today, we have to also worry about videographers because, apparently, it's not enough to just have still pictures that you will hardly ever look at. No, in this modern, fast-paced world you'll also need a live-action video that you will pay just as much for (and look at even less).

Think about it. Other than "Field of Dreams" and "Tin Cup," how many movies do you watch over and over again? In truth, probably not many. In fact, even the best movies wear thin after you've seen them two or three times. Yet, despite the fact you will probably pay enough for your wedding video to fund a low-budget movie, yours is not going to be nearly as entertaining. Face it, there are only so many times you can watch "Star Wars" or "Avatar," or even that ground ball going through Buckner's legs if you're Mets fan, and even fewer times you can watch your drunken relatives stumble around dancing and giving you advice on marriage. Still, your wife and relatives are going to insist you need a video. (But, hey, maybe you'll get lucky and capture a moment that will go viral on YouTube. You know, like you passing out at the altar or something along those lines....)

As for picking the videographer, most of the rules for a photographer also hold true. Obviously, the cheapest choice is to have a friend shoot the video. It may not be "professional quality," but with the money you save you'll be able to buy something really useful, like a nice big grill or a pickup truck. And keep in mind that some photographers will only work with certain videographers so, if you want that photographer, you may have one less choice to make (which isn't really a bad thing).

But, if you don't have a friend who will do the dirty work, and/ or your photographer doesn't have a teammate, then all you have to do is ask other married friends, or at least friends who know married people, because friends are happy to offer suggestions. It makes them feel useful and that you owe them. Just follow the same "things to avoid" from the previous section and you will be fine.

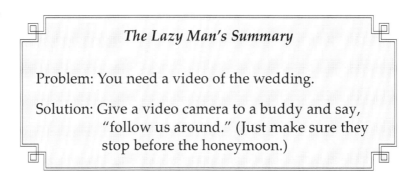

The Lazy Man's Summary

Problem: You need a video of the wedding.

Solution: Give a video camera to a buddy and say, "follow us around." (Just make sure they stop before the honeymoon.)

The band / music

Picking the music for your wedding isn't as easy as you'd think. (Are you sensing a pattern, yet?) But, luckily, it's also not quite as complicated as other parts of the wedding because this is something you may at least be able to comprehend.

In general, the music is broken up into two parts:

➢ Music for the ceremony

➢ Music for the reception

Music for the ceremony is usually fairly traditional. This is good because once again it means less thinking on your part. There is the wedding march (the "here comes the bride song") and a few others that will probably be played at your wedding, either on an organ (a big fancy piano) or something similar. Don't sweat it. It will sound fine.

Music for the reception, however, can be a bit trickier as there are many more possibilities, starting with who provides the tunes. So, here's some options, from cheapest to probably most expensive:

1. Bring your own CDs and MP3s and have your friends bring theirs to simply play at the wedding. Sure, this may not be the "coolest" way to do it, but it is inexpensive and practical.

2. Hire a DJ to pay somebody for what your friends could do for free. The advantage to this method is you don't have to inconvenience one or more of

your buddies. Plus, the DJ should, in theory, have a larger selection than what's on your iPod and better equipment, too—like speakers.

3. Hire a band. Bands have the advantage that they are live, add a nice personal feel, and can insert energy into the party. But because bands are live, you can never be certain what you are getting. The singer could bite the head off a bat, for example, or the lead guitarist could set his instrument on fire. Or they could just stink. And CDs don't have days off, take breaks, or have one (or two) too many while on break (which is where word of mouth—or ear—comes into play). If you know of a band that's getting good reviews, then it may very well be worth the cost. Some bands also have demo tapes you can listen to.

4. Some combination of 2 and 3, or hiring more than one band. This way you are sort of covered for all occasions—but it's going to cost you.

One aspect you may have thought a little about is *your song*. Not "Your Song," but *your song*; the song that makes you and your bride think of each other when you hear it. A song that should have some sort of meaning for you both (which means Meatloaf's "Bat Out of Hell" is probably out of the question).

For instance, one of the authors and his bride picked "Kiss the Girl" from the *Little Mermaid* (but he's still macho—honest). The reason they picked the song was simple: the *Little Mermaid* movie was their first date and the first time they kissed. So, it was a natural choice. (They even named their son after the crab in the movie. It's not only cute, but now it gives them something to taunt him with.)

And if it helps, the other author and his bride picked Kermit the Frog singing "Rainbow Connection." (They did not, however, name either of their sons after Muppets.)

Of course, overall, this is pretty much between you and your bride (you can bet she will have an opinion on this). As long as whatever you two choose has meaning to both of you, it will be fine so, with that in mind, here are some hints:

➢ Avoid the theme from *Rocky*

➢ Avoid beer jingles

➢ Avoid any song by 50 Cent

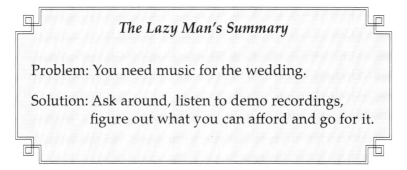

The Lazy Man's Summary

Problem: You need music for the wedding.

Solution: Ask around, listen to demo recordings, figure out what you can afford and go for it.

The meal

Finally, we're talking about something you're good at—eating. As with cake, you've been choosing and eating your own food for a long time and probably have it down by now; as a result, it's very likely your fiancée will bow to your wisdom, or at the very least listen to your opinion. The thing to remember is, for this meal you are planning for a lot of other people. What might be great for you might not work out at all for a few hundred of your closest friends, especially when you are footing the bill for all these fine folks.

In the past, wedding meals used to be simple, either some kind of chicken or some kind meat, or maybe a choice of either. Toss in a vegetable and a salad and you're good to go. Today, it's not that simple. Now you need a veggie choice for those who don't eat meat, and with the growing popularity of low-carb diets, you may want to have a trendy low-carb choice. Plus, everybody always wants to outdo everybody else, or at the very least do something different with the food at their wedding. So, even if you go with some sort of chicken or some sort of meat, you will quickly learn there are many,

many, many sorts of either. The choices can be mind-boggling, and that's even before considering if it should be a sit-down dinner, with one or more courses, or a buffet, or something different (don't ask what, but you can bet somebody will come up with something) .

To make this as easy as sinking a six-inch putt, we'll cut through all the selection criteria and hyperbole and get to the two most important points in picking a wedding meal:

> Pick something you like to eat. Heck, it's your wedding. It's only natural. You're a guy, you like to eat; it's one of the few things in life you are really, really good at. Sure, your fiancée knows lots of stuff like what temperature chicken is done at and what fork to use, and where (and where not) to put your elbows, and when to belch — but you know how to eat! She has to give way to your level of expertise.

> Pick something affordable. Yes, lobster is great and it would make for a memorable meal, but lobster for a hundred and fifty guests can be a year's mortgage.

Also take note that even if you are not paying, you should consider the feelings and pocketbooks of the people who are. After all, you may need a loan from them someday and you don't want them saying, "Sorry, but the two tons of lobster we paid for at your wedding really put the pinch on our bank account..." Remember, people who pay for weddings have feelings and limited bank accounts also.[7]

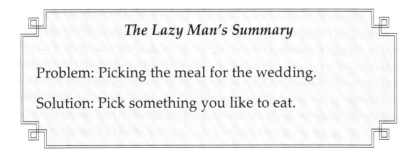

The Lazy Man's Summary

Problem: Picking the meal for the wedding.

Solution: Pick something you like to eat.

---

7 Unless you are marrying a Trump, Gates, Kardashian, or Hilton (but that comes with its own unique set of problems). *Also see footnote 1.*

The seating

The peace talks to end World War II were probably pulled off with less stress than the seating arrangements for your wedding will be as your fiancée (and you) will not only have to worry about who sits at what table, but who sits with whom as well.

Considering the big picture, you (being a guy and fairly clueless) would naturally think this is minor stuff, and that people would just shrug it off and deal with it wherever they happen to be seated; however, you couldn't be more wrong.

Seems there is some sort of unwritten family hierarchy that must be followed when placing people at tables and, apparently, the closer to the bride and groom's table one is seated, the more prestigious a table is. Therefore, certain relatives and friends might be a bit peeved if they don't get what they consider to be a "primo" table.

Another problem is that some people will want to sit next to certain people—and as far away from other certain people as possible. Once again, this could take the skills of a UN negotiator and a statistician to weigh through all the options and permutations.

For instance, say that crazy Uncle Bob wants to sit across from Aunt Sally and Aunt Amy, but he doesn't want to see Uncle Sal. Uncle Sal doesn't want to sit by Uncle Bob either but would like to be near the bar. Aunt Sally for her part likes to sit between Uncle Bob and Uncle Sal because she enjoys seeing them fight. While Aunt Amy wants nothing to do with either Bob or Sal, but winks a lot at Aunt Sally. Needless to say, it won't be easy. And you probably won't make everybody happy. But, whatever happens, just make sure that you and your bride are happy.

And, sometimes, there is even the urge in some to try to play matchmaker and make certain people sit near each other just because they might "hit it off...." For example, your bride thinks her friend Susie (you know, the one with the "great personality") and your cousin, Matt, would get along perfectly, so they should sit at the same table. You, of course, being the guy, realize Matt is a guy and that Matt doesn't give three cents about personality. He would much rather sit by your wife's hot friend Tatiana. What do you do?

Well, if you like Matt a lot, you could always try to position him between the two girls and see how things shake out.... (Hey, just because you're getting married doesn't mean Matt can't have some fun now, right?)

Anyway, the best solution is often just to let your fiancée handle it. Not because you are lazy or a coward but because she, being a woman, probably has a bit more finesse than you when it comes to this kind of stuff. Remember, women are naturally nurturing, while men are more into winning than mediating. Well, this is exactly the type of situation where you can't win, so a mediator is called for.

(FYI, you could always have "open seating" for everyone who wasn't in the wedding party. Call it "survival of the fittest" seating—hey, it could be entertaining to watch people jockey for position. Now, you probably won't be able to convince your wife this is good, but if you catch her in the right mood you might get lucky....)

 Note: If your family, or worse, both of your families, are beset by divorce, be aware your seating woes will be infinitely more difficult. If this is the case, you will be forced to just hope and pray a lot.

Your bride's gift

You'd think that $5,000 engagement ring and you alone would be gift enough for your bride; however, in some cases it just doesn't cut it. Some couples like to exchange gifts, either before, during, or right after the wedding. (Guess they think of it as another way to cement their love.)

Yet, with all the stuff you have to do planning and paying for a wedding, you really don't need to be spending a whole lot of time and money planning and buying gifts for each other, too. Your wedding day will (probably) already be the happiest day of your life, so you should save the gift giving for a time when you could both use a little pick-me-up.

Still, you know your bride-to-be best (at least you should). Therefore, it's up to you to decide if she'd be especially pleased with you buying her a wedding present.

So make note that if she says any of the following key phrases, it usually means you'd better start shopping:

> "You're going to love what I bought you for the wedding." *This translates to: "I hope I love what you bought me."*

> "Oh, you don't have to buy me anything for the wedding." *This translates to: "Yes, you do," because this is a crafty way of saying something and meaning the exact opposite. This is something you'll encounter over and over and over throughout your married life. (If you can't understand it, at least learn to accept it.)*

> "What do you want from me as your wedding gift? *This translates to: "I'm buying you something so I expect the same."*

> "You'd better buy me a nice wedding gift!" *If this needs translating you are in big trouble. You're way too dense to get married. Go buy a nice dog; it'll love you no matter what.*

If you must buy a gift, take these factors into account:

> ➤ Your financial situation. Don't put yourself into debt unless your bride would really want you to —not over a gift anyway. A house you both pick out together, maybe. As a symbolic after-we-get-married gesture, think again.

> ➤ Your bride's likes and dislikes. Remember, your bride is probably a woman and, therefore, has some different (and very specific) likes and dislikes. So, while you may consider an Xbox a great gift, she might not (unless she does really like Halo).

> ➤ It's also probably not such a hot idea to buy clothing. Not only is it so "last century," most men usually have no idea what actually fits women. And the last thing you want to do is guess and be wrong.

> ➤ You can never go wrong with jewelry. Just ask the clerk at the counter of the jewelry store for help.

How to discover your bride's likes and dislikes

(By the way, while you should already know some of the answers, it's good to have confirmation, so you might want to actually ask her these questions then write down her answers for later reference.)

> ➤ What's your favorite color?

> ➤ What's your favorite kind of jewelry?

> ➤ What's your birthstone?

> ➤ What's your favorite kind of music?

> ➤ What's your favorite show?

> ➤ What's your favorite season?

> ➤ What's your favorite city?

> ➤ What's your favorite food?

> ➤ What's your favorite pet?

> ➤ What's your favorite drink?

> ➤ Are you allergic to anything?

> ➤ Is there anything you absolutely don't like?

> Q. A groom who is marrying you should spend _____ on a wedding gift for you, his bride:

>> A) 0$ - $25   B) $26 - $50

>> C) $100 to $500   D) More than $1,000

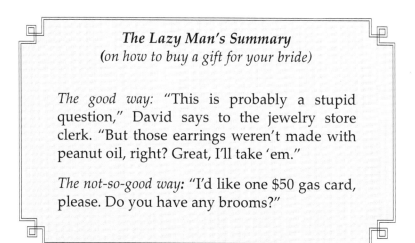

The Lazy Man's Summary
(on how to buy a gift for your bride)

The good way: "This is probably a stupid question," David says to the jewelry store clerk. "But those earrings weren't made with peanut oil, right? Great, I'll take 'em."

The not-so-good way: "I'd like one $50 gas card, please. Do you have any brooms?"

Your wedding party's gift

It's traditional to buy gifts for the members of your wedding party. These mementoes give them something to remember your wedding by (in case they get drunk and can't remember anything else). Yet, unless you own Microsoft, a fancy hotel, or host a reality show, they don't have to be big gifts—more like tokens of your appreciation. Standard gifts are things like mugs, pens, cuff links, and other random little items. There are even websites that specialize in, or at least sell, individualized wedding trinkets, so you don't even have to leave the house. (Aren't modern times wonderful? Poor cavemen grooms probably had to go out and kill then skin their presents.)

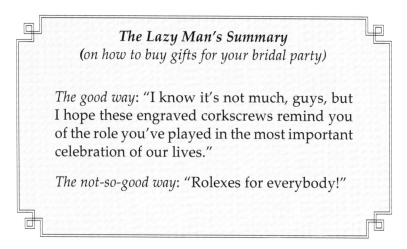

The Lazy Man's Summary
(on how to buy gifts for your bridal party)

The good way: "I know it's not much, guys, but I hope these engraved corkscrews remind you of the role you've played in the most important celebration of our lives."

The not-so-good way: "Rolexes for everybody!"

Your honeymoon

If you are planning a honeymoon for right after your wedding, you and your bride should probably have the spot picked out at least a month or two in advance. This probably won't be that tough, as there are some brides who have known where they wanted to honeymoon since they were five. (If your bride is one of these types, don't try to fight it. You can't win. Just go where she wants.)

But, if your bride is open to suggestions, any of the traditional kind of places like those listed below will work fine. Just use this handy reference table for a list of pros and notes. (In essence, there aren't any cons to a honeymoon location because you will be "on your honeymoon" and no matter what you do, it'll be fun.)

Picking the Honeymoon Spot

Place	Pros	Notes
Niagara Falls	A classic choice with many scenic views.	You'll be on your honeymoon and probably don't need a lot of scenic views.
Vegas	Lots to do all the time. Food can be cheap.	If you are pushing for Vegas don't use the line, "But, honey, there are a lot of hot women there...."
Hawaii	Great weather, great people, great food.	Not a good choice if you are afraid of flying, unless of course you already live in Hawaii.
Paris	A classy choice; a romantic city.	Pretend not to be an American.
		(cont...)

The Grand Canyon	Different than most would choose; one of the wonders of our country.	This pick is best left to those nature types.
Costa Rica	Great weather, great people, great food.	While Costa Rica may be considered a third-world country, it is quite advanced with a good medical system and cable TV. There is a rainy season and Spanish is the native tongue.
The Bahamas	It's the Bahamas.	Becoming a trendy pick.
Any of the Disney Parks	A good choice if you never got to go as a kid.	As interesting as his lecture may be, listening to Lincoln drone on in the Hall of Presidents may not leave your bride in the mood for love.
A Cruise	Everything you want in a giant hotel that moves from place to place.	Hey, they've had at least two Love Boat TV series about cruise ships. If it's good enough to be on TV, then it's good enough for you.

(The keen observer will probably note that many of these same spots were also listed on the special places to get married chart. Well, duh.)

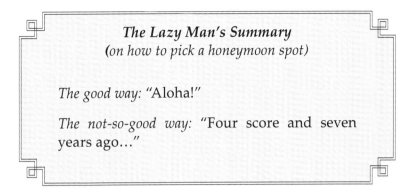

The Lazy Man's Summary
(on how to pick a honeymoon spot)

The good way: "Aloha!"

The not-so-good way: "Four score and seven years ago..."

Wedding planners

The wedding planner is another phenomenon of modern times. Seeing how planning for a wedding can be a royal pain in the butt, of course somebody found a way to profit from of it. Yet, wedding planners have the advantage in taking some of the searching and thinking (and worrying) away from your bride and you.

However, wedding planners have the disadvantage in that they are yet another thing to pay for. Plus, some wedding planners can be as hard to deal with as in-laws. Others may even think they are more essential to the wedding than say, you.

Still, if the wedding planning is turning out to be even worse than you expected, and you have some extra cash, you may want to consider this option. After all, dealing with a bitchy wedding planner for a few weeks is a LOT better than dealing with a bitchy future wife for the next forty-plus years.

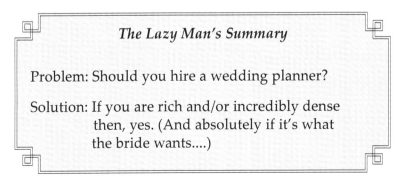

The Lazy Man's Summary

Problem: Should you hire a wedding planner?

Solution: If you are rich and/or incredibly dense then, yes. (And absolutely if it's what the bride wants....)

Get Your Game Face On 4

Cold feet

At some time during this entire process you are going to find yourself wondering if you are doing the right thing. Your thought process may even resemble the following:

"Oh, my God. Oh, my God!!!"

"What the hell am I going?"

"I'm committing to one person for the rest of my life!"

"Do I want to be with one person for the rest of my life?"

"What if she decides she doesn't want to be with me?"

"I mean, hell, I'm a great guy, but I've been told I have one or two teeny tiny flaws. Those might get on her nerves after a while. Then what?"

"Sleeping with one woman—forever!! What if she gets fat?"

"What if I get fat?"

"Oh, man, I gotta call it off. I wonder if we'll get our money back on the rings?"

"Oh, man, she'll hate me."

"Is love really forever? I thought I'd love my first car forever, but when I got my second car, I forgot about my first car. Why the hell am I thinking about cars?"

"Oh, my God! Oh, my God!! Oh, my God!!!"

Usually you will have these thoughts late at night or when you're stuck in traffic or any time you have too much time on your hands. But don't worry; these thoughts are perfectly normal. Almost everybody (yes, even your fiancée) has them. It stems from the idea that while change may be good, change isn't always easy. You've probably been single and able to come and go as you please for most of your adult life—and now that's going to change. But hard as it may be to believe from time to time, it is a change for the better. You're going from a "you" to a "we." From the moment you say those vows, you'll have a partner in life. Somebody to pick you up when you are down and to let you know when you screw up. Life will be better—not perfect, but better. Just remember that and you'll be fine. However, even with that said, there are a few cold feet-type thoughts you may want to pay attention to, such as:

> *"Oh, my God! I'm going to miss 'Glee' for this!"*
>
> *"Damn, that bridesmaid is hot! I wonder what's she's up to tomorrow night?"*
>
> *"Maybe we can get married and I can still date other chicks…?"*

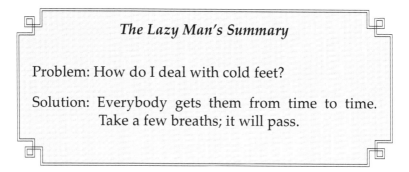

The Lazy Man's Summary

Problem: How do I deal with cold feet?

Solution: Everybody gets them from time to time. Take a few breaths; it will pass.

Fighting

Every couple fights. Even the famous ones—Romeo and Juliet, Sonny and Cher, Jay Z and Beyonce—fight. Even during times of low stress people tend to fight. So, it's inevitable that on occasion two people who have one goal in mind but different objectives on how to reach the goal will fight. Or that two people may hold conflicting views over the limited resources needed to reach their goals. Or two people may have totally distinct goals. Heck, two people may just get off on fighting because they like fighting.

The thing is, all couples fight. And with the stress of the wedding, there will be times when you are going to argue. She's going to get on your nerves and, believe it or not, you might even get on hers. It's bound to happen, but as long as it's not something you are doing all the time, it might actually be a good way to get stuff off both your chests (and can actually be exhilarating for some couples).

Therefore, if there's something really eating at you, or if you just plain feel like fighting for a bit (for we all know make-up sex can be great), then prepare to argue. Don't go off the deep end too far or she might not throw you a lifesaver, but do state your point clearly and make your case by supporting your point with as many facts (or pseudo-facts) as you can. But remember to be flexible. Flexibility and opposable thumbs are what separates us from the animals. It also doesn't hurt to tell your fiancée your feelings. Yes, like it or not, you do have some feelings. No, you don't have to get all mushy or anything, but women like to know how men feel. So, in this case, feelings are good. It shows you have a sensitive side. Plus, nobody likes to hurt the feelings of somebody they love.

But if you do fight, bear in mind there is no reason (or excuse) to be insulting. If you stoop to that level, you'd probably lose an insult battle anyhow. (Be honest, you have a lot more flaws than she does.) Also, there's never a reason to get physical (hey, you'll get hurt too — women naturally fight dirty and have a higher threshold for pain).

It also pays to take into account that men and women are different. Yes, you're going to be married soon, so you'll need to know this stuff now, even if you're already thinking, "I know women are different! My wife has great boobs and I don't! Plus, I have something she doesn't!" But these differences are more than just physical. You have to understand that women's brains are literally wired differently, and they have different levels of hormones then men. This means they both think and act differently, which is important because this means that both men and woman will have different arguing and problem-solving styles.

Think about it: Women are gatherers. They are built on cooperation— working together toward a common goal. Plus, women are the traditional child bearers, so they are typically more nurturing. But, push them hard enough and they can be neutering (which is something you don't want them to even think about). Women, being who they are as women, usually like to work together to find solutions (preferably one that gels with their original idea, of course).

Men, however, are wired mentally and hormonally to be "hunters." Back a few million years ago, we needed to hunt down our dinner to survive. We haven't really evolved much over the last few million years and that means we still tend toward the more aggressive side. You've probably noticed we'll compete over anything. Who can spit farther. Who can belch louder. You name it; we'll make a competition out of it. This competitive side may play a role while we compete for mates, but you're getting married now so the competitive side needs to be reined in (at least when dealing with your fiancée).

It also doesn't help that men like to win, which is all fine and dandy when you are hunting down a saber-toothed tiger for dinner but, the thing is, we no longer need to hunt down our dinner for our survival. We have pizza delivery people to do it for us.

So, while we are still wired to be hunters like our ancestors, the times have changed, yet our brains haven't caught up with the times. (Which is why we have sports to help us unleash some of that competitive energy on somebody we don't have to live with for the rest of our lives.)

So, you need to remember that while competition is good, marriage isn't a sport. Your bride-to-be is your partner, your mate, even your teammate—but not your competition.

This means when you argue, you keep an open mind and fight fair. You remind yourself that every argument has two sides and, as right as you may think you are, surely there is some merit in what your fiancée has to say. Look for the merit. Find a common-ground solution that works for you both. If you do that, then more than likely you both will win.

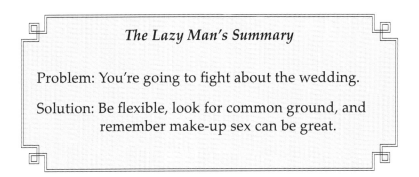

Stress

Your wedding day is meant to be one of the happiest days of your life, if not the happiest. (Yes, even happier than the time you scored that winning touchdown.) Therefore, planning for it is going to be very stressful, and your fiancée (thus, you) will have a lot to plan for and worry about. The list can be long and includes, but is certainly not limited to:

➤ Finding the right gown. (Your bride will probably/ hopefully be more worried about this than you.)

➤ What if my tux doesn't fit?

➤ What if I forget to invite my mother?

➤ What if I accidentally invite Lex Luthor?

➤ Are the invitations the right color and font?

➤ Will I offend anybody by not having them in the wedding party?

➤ Will anybody I pick for the wedding party offend anybody else?

➤ What if the meal isn't good or the meat is tainted?

➤ What if the priest/reverend/preacher/justice of the peace/boat captain gets sick or changes careers and can't make it?

> ➤ What if the place where we're holding the reception gets destroyed by a flood, meteor strike, or other act of God?

> ➤ What if my feet stink?

> ➤ What if my in-laws turn out to be even more giant pains in the butt than I thought?

> ➤ Am I doing the right thing?

> ➤ What if the band's lead singer gets wasted and hits on my mother in-law?

> ➤ What if my mother in-law gets wasted and hits on the band's lead singer, or worse yet, the drummer?

> ➤ What if it rains/snows (yes, even in June) or is too sunny?

Basically, the point is, if it can be worried about, chances are very good your fiancée—therefore, you—will worry about it. And once you're married, things won't be quite the same again, which only adds to the pressure and stress of making sure this whole shindig goes off without a hitch. Still, you can handle it. You have to remember most of the pressure is "made up pressure." No lives are hanging in the balance. You are not landing a plane without any landing gear. You're not storming the beach at Normandy. You're not up in the bottom of the ninth in Game 7 of the World Series with two outs, two strikes, a man on third, and your team down two runs.

Murphy's Law states: *Anything that can go wrong will go wrong.* This is especially applicable during wedding times. It just is. So, the only way to fight this is to not fight it. You just have to go with Zakour/Schading law, which states: *Don't worry, it will work out.*

Okay, it's not really a law. But Murphy's Law isn't really a law either. The key is not to sweat the little things too much. Of course, this is much easier said than done, but just remember this simple mantra: *No matter what goes wrong, we will still get married and people will still enjoy themselves at the wedding.*

Sure, the statement's not all that catchy, but it drives the point across of how the silly little details of planning a wedding sometimes get in the way of the bigger picture. Your wedding should just be a time for your fiancée and you and some of your friends and family to get together so you and your fiancée can commit to each other. All the other things are nice, but they're not really all that important in the long run. So don't sweat it. Things will work out.

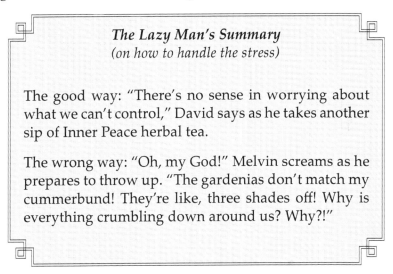

The Lazy Man's Summary
(on how to handle the stress)

The good way: "There's no sense in worrying about what we can't control," David says as he takes another sip of Inner Peace herbal tea.

The wrong way: "Oh, my God!" Melvin screams as he prepares to throw up. "The gardenias don't match my cummerbund! They're like, three shades off! Why is everything crumbling down around us? Why?!"

What to say (a lot)

During all stages of the wedding, things might get—as noted often so it will sink in—stressful. This stress will range from anywhere from a little to a lot. Once again, it's important to remain calm and not to say anything stupid. (Of course, this might not be easy for you for sometimes we guys just don't know what is stupid and what isn't.) To help, here is a list of phrases to use when things get tight:

"I love you so much."
"I don't deserve you. "
"Let me know how I can help."
"Let's have sex." (It's worth a shot.)
"It looks like you could use some shopping time."
"Things are going to work out just fine."
"I'm so glad you are a part of my life."
"Let's have kinky sex." (It's still worth a shot.)
"Let's go out and have a nice romantic dinner."

"You are so beautiful."
"You are so smart."
"You are so hot."
"Have you lost weight?"
"Our love is the important thing."
"Let me cook (or order) dinner."
"Need a foot rub?"
"It will be beautiful."

But, before using any of these, just make sure you listen carefully (or at least more than usual) to avoid saying it out of context.

What not to say

While planning the wedding, things will be tense from time to time (okay, most of the time)—yet, don't make things worse; try to avoid saying any of the following phrases:

"Quiet, the game is on!"
"My mother says you should...."
"Let's go to Hooters for lunch."
"Let's have the rehearsal dinner at Hooters."
"Yesterday, at Hooters...."
"Have you ever considered breast implants?"
"Are you gaining weight?"
"You know your mom's a bitch."
"Is it that time of the month again?"
"Boy, your dad is an ass."
"That's a bad day to get married, I have a bowling match."
"No! Not that day! There's an Adam Sandler marathon on!"
"Do my feet smell as bad as I think they do?"
"You're wearing white?"
"How many of my old girlfriends can I invite?"

The in-laws

Sure, you're a great guy, but don't be surprised if your in-laws have trouble warming up to you—after all, as much as their daughter may have been a pain in their collective butts when growing up, she is still their daughter and *the light of their lives.* There's just no way you're going to be good enough for their little girl.

Of course, your father-in-law is going to have a hard time with you. Why? Because you are, or will be, the man sleeping with his daughter. Hey, all fathers want to believe their daughters are virgins, even after they've given birth to their fifth kid. It's just how fathers are. You'll have to deal with it. Just smile and nod a lot and say, "Yes, sir." Hopefully, he's not too much bigger than you are and you can eventually bond (to the point where he considers you still not worthy of his daughter but higher than say, pond scum) over common points of reference like sports and beer. (Steer clear of talking about women.)

The mother-in-law is a different creature, seeing that your fiancée probably drove her crazy growing up and now it's payback time. Her daughter is getting married, which means if all goes according to her plans, she'll soon be a grandma (a young and vital grandma). This means she can't really take out her frustration on her childbearing daughter, so she will in turn take it out on the next best thing—you. Hopefully, again, she's not too much bigger than you are and you can find some sort of common point to bond over.

Brothers-in-law are a different type of creature altogether. There are the over-protective types who believe, "You're not nearly good enough for our sister." Then they will take every opportunity to pound you into the ground during any family sporting event. (You'd better hope you are either faster, smarter or bigger.) And don't worry, after a few years of taking their pounding, they will probably grow to accept you (or simply tire of you) and pound on you less.

Then there is the opposite extreme, brothers-in-law who care nothing about their sister. Usually these guys just care either about what you can do for them (for example, drywall) or how your coming into the family will inconvenience them. If you just ignore them, or treat them as mostly harmless, they will eventually leave you alone.

Sisters-in-law are another story. They come in all shapes and sizes. There are even the "just plain evil ones" who enjoy causing trouble. They may flirt with you, just for kicks, as a test of your faithfulness. If you don't play their game, they will tire of you too (heck, you're really not that great) and move on to somebody new to taunt.

Then there are the "jealous ones." These would be the sisters who believe your fiancée is the spoiled one and gets all the good stuff, while they get the leftovers and hand-me-downs. It doesn't matter if what they believe is true or not; they're going to *think* it's true so that's all that matters. The good things about these types of sisters-in-law is they usually take out most of their aggression (be it passive or true aggression) on your fiancée. Your job is to be supportive of your fiancée while also trying to not totally alienate the sister-in-law. Say stuff like, "Your feelings are valid..." and you should be okay.

Next there is the "know-it-all" sister-in-law. She is either older than your wife or just thinks she's older due to "life experiences." These are the ones who are experts in everything. They also feel you're a man so you can't know all that much. These women may mean well, but they can be gigantic pains in the butt. If this is yours, simply nod your head a lot and say, "Ah, I see."

Finally, there is the "bitter unmarried" sister-in-law type. She may be divorced, she may be gay, she may have never found "the right guy," but whatever the reason, she is alone and you're not surprised. She's the type who can suck the energy out of a room like a vampire—and for all you know, she may very well be one. Your best bet is to give her a lot of space.

 It's possible to find a brother- or sister-in-law to be no trouble, but it's not that probable, and certainly not as much fun to write about.

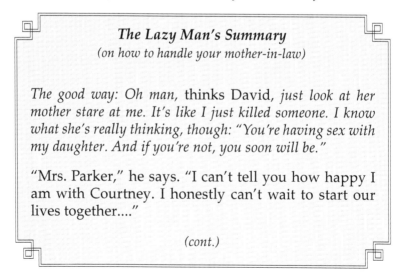

The Lazy Man's Summary
(on how to handle your mother-in-law)

The good way: Oh man, thinks David, *just look at her mother stare at me. It's like I just killed someone. I know what she's really thinking, though: "You're having sex with my daughter. And if you're not, you soon will be."*

"Mrs. Parker," he says. "I can't tell you how happy I am with Courtney. I honestly can't wait to start our lives together...."

(cont.)

> ### The Lazy Man's Summary
> *(on how to handle your mother-in-law cont.)*
>
> *The not-so-good way: Oh man,* thinks Melvin, *just look at her mother stare at me. It's like I just killed someone. I know what she's really thinking, though: "You're having sex with my daughter. And if you're not, you soon will be."*
>
> "Mrs. Peterson, I can tell you're uncomfortable because you think I'm having red hot sweaty monkey sex with your daughter," Melvin says.
>
> Mrs. Peterson's jaw falls slack.
>
> "But I just want to assure you I am not, in fact, having red hot sweaty monkey SEX with your daughter," says Melvin. "Although...I certainly hope to do just that after we are properly married!"
>
> Regardless of what they're actually doing, he thinks he's telling the old bird exactly what she wants to hear...well, more or less, anyway.
>
> *The just plain terrible way: Oh man,* thinks Melvin, *just look at her mother stare at me. It's like I just killed someone. I know what she's really thinking, though: "You're having sex with my daughter. And if you're not, you soon will be."*
>
> "Mrs. Peterson, I had no idea your daughter was such sex kitten." Melvin says. "You wouldn't believe what she asked me to do just before we came over here...."

Your parents

While your fiancée's parents are naturally going to think you're not good enough for her, *your* parents won't be quite so predictable. Fathers of the groom (for the most part) are just going to be happy their sons are getting married because this shows you're (probably) not gay, therefore, they did their job raising you. And a few dads may even try to hit on your fiancée, but this is usually nothing to worry about. It's just your dad trying to gain back a bit of his youth through you. (Think of it as a compliment.)

However, moms are more unpredictable. For instance, some might be shocked that anybody would marry you; although, they'll be happy somebody so much more civilized than you would have you. Others are the old *"Everybody Loves Raymond"* type of moms (look it up it if you don't know). They will look at your wife as just a substitute for her—a pale, almost transparent substitute, at best. These types of moms can drive your bride crazy as they will make it clear to her (either passively or obviously) that her only purpose and worth in life is to bear your children—and her grandchildren.

Still, none of this matters all that much to you because they are your parents. You've known them all your life and you are used to their little idiosyncrasies. However, just remember, while you may be used to them, your wife isn't. Plus, when you think about it, your sweet dear mom *is* her "evil mother-in-law...."

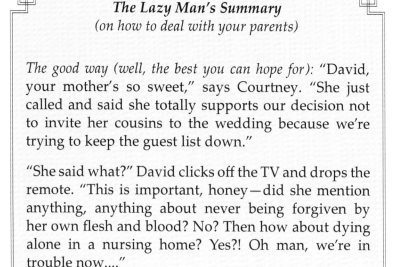

The Lazy Man's Summary
(on how to deal with your parents)

The good way (well, the best you can hope for): "David, your mother's so sweet," says Courtney. "She just called and said she totally supports our decision not to invite her cousins to the wedding because we're trying to keep the guest list down."

"She said what?" David clicks off the TV and drops the remote. "This is important, honey—did she mention anything, anything about never being forgiven by her own flesh and blood? No? Then how about dying alone in a nursing home? Yes?! Oh man, we're in trouble now...."

(cont.)

> ### The Lazy Man's Summary
> #### (on how to deal with your parents cont.)
>
> *The not-so-good way:* "Melvin, your mother just called and said she's not at all concerned about the seating arrangements and wouldn't even care if she ended up next to your father," says Shanice.
>
> "Terrific!" says Melvin. "I've been a little concerned those two might have some trouble even being in the same city together. I mean, it's been more than twenty years. Did I ever tell you the story about my kindergarten graduation? Boy, I didn't think the paramedics would ever get there...."

Your unmarried guy friends

Now that you are getting married, your unmarried guy friends are either going to be envious of you, pity you, or be stuck somewhere in between. The other interesting phenomenon is that they will all give you advice on marriage.

Yes, apparently some of your unmarried friends believe the fact that no woman has taken them makes them an expert on marriage. Therefore, they must share their wisdom with you. This can be related to going to a doctor who has never performed a vasectomy and having them perform a vasectomy—on you. Sure, it could work out, but wouldn't you feel better having the operation done by somebody who has successfully performed a vasectomy—or seventy? Of course you would.

So, go ahead, listen to your unmarried guy friends drone on about how marriage should be, but don't pay too much attention to it. Remember, your unmarried friends are more likely than not to be unmarried because most women probably find them repulsive, so don't put too much stock in anything they say about women (unless, of course, your unmarried guy friends are gay, in which case you should pay very close attention).

Plus, be aware that your unmarried friends may also try to get you to go out and party with them. Sure, you can do this, but be smart about it, and don't let them talk you into doing anything stupid. Remember, if these guys were actually as bright as they thought they were they would have all married rich babes by now.

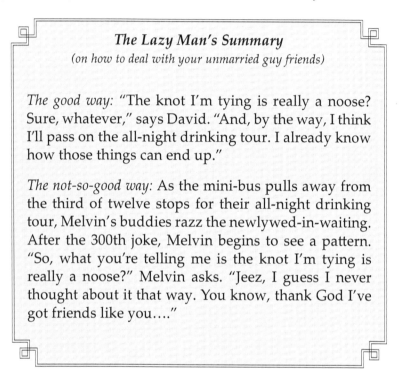

The Lazy Man's Summary
(on how to deal with your unmarried guy friends)

The good way: "The knot I'm tying is really a noose? Sure, whatever," says David. "And, by the way, I think I'll pass on the all-night drinking tour. I already know how those things can end up."

The not-so-good way: As the mini-bus pulls away from the third of twelve stops for their all-night drinking tour, Melvin's buddies razz the newlywed-in-waiting. After the 300th joke, Melvin begins to see a pattern. "So, what you're telling me is the knot I'm tying is really a noose?" Melvin asks. "Jeez, I guess I never thought about it that way. You know, thank God I've got friends like you...."

Your married guy friends

(Remember them? The ones you haven't seen since their wedding days?)

Your married guy friends are going to welcome you to the club for soon you will be one of them. You share a bond, a knowledge, a trust. It's kind of like being in a frat, but without the secret handshakes and stuff. Your married guy friends will also feel it is their duty to impart their wisdom on you. The catch is not all your married friends are happy with their marriages. Some may even be downright depressed and, therefore, depressing. The trick is to figure out which buddies those are, for the ones who seem happy may not really be, and those who don't seem too happy might actually be.

There is an example of two couples who were married about the same time. One couple always appeared to be fighting; the other was always all lovey-dovey. Notice the word *was*.

As it turned out, the latter couple is now no longer a couple, while the former is still hanging in there. Remember, not all marriages are created equal and what works for one couple may not work for you. Heck, that's why marriage counselors exist and make all sorts of money.

The Lazy Man's Summary
(on how to deal with your married guy friends)

The good way: "Listen, man, you're going to fight. You're going to bicker. Get used to it. Remember, you're both human. You both make mistakes. As long as there are more good times than bad, you're going to be okay," says Kyle, David's friend since kindergarten, and well into his third year of marriage, something of an expert on the ups and downs of the blessed union.

David takes the conversation to heart but keeps in mind that for every relationship there are different problems—and different solutions....

The not-so-good way: "Listen, when she gets angry, just go watch TV. Granted, it will make her angrier, but by then you can consider yourself winning the argument. And, remember, when she yells at you for keeping score, don't forget to point out who's winning."

Melvin is always grateful when Big Dan offers advice, for with three marriages under his belt at the ripe old age of 34, it must mean Dan is something of an expert.

"Dan-O, my man," says Melvin. "Why those chicks didn't appreciate you, I'll never know...."

Your ex-girlfriends

This is the easiest section in the book to write. Some old girlfriends, who never used to hold any interest, will suddenly find you extremely attractive now that somebody else wants you. Dealing with them is easy — don't. Avoid them at all costs. Nothing good, besides a slight ego boost, can come of it. As for inviting ex-girlfriends to your wedding, you can do it — but you can also play Russian roulette with a loaded gun, and neither is a good idea.

The Lazy Man's Summary
(on how to deal with an ex-girlfriend)

The good way: "Hi, David, it's Jennifer."

The voice on the other end is disturbingly familiar. "Jealous Jennifer" has reared that proverbial "ugly head" of hers once again.

Of course, in strictly physical terms, the word ugly has never been used to describe Jennifer "Too Hot" Hemminger.

"Just thought I'd say hi," she purrs. "I heard you're getting married — how exciting! I still say you should have married me, though. Especially since you know how good I look on the beach."

David is speechless. She had dumped him because of her suspicions about him seeing another woman on the side. Granted, he was — but that woman was his mother, and she was in the hospital at the time.

"I'm sorry, I have to go," David says. "My mother's the hospital again. And she's gonna be there a while!"

(cont.)

The Lazy Man's Summary
(on how to deal with an ex-girlfriend cont.)

The not-so-good way: "Hi, Melvin, it's Jessica."

The voice on the other end is disturbingly familiar. "Jealous Jessica" has reared her proverbial "ugly head" once again. Of course, in strictly physical terms, the word ugly has never been used to describe Jessica "Too Hot" Johnson.

"Just thought I'd say hi," she purrs. "I heard you're getting married—how exciting! I still say you should have married me, though. Especially since you know how good I look on the beach."

"Hot damn!" Melvin yells. "Shanice, I'm gonna need that ring back...!"

The Big Game   5

The rehearsal

A day or two before the wedding, you may be asked to rehearse. This is going to be like the real wedding, but without the pomp and circumstance and uncomfortable clothing. This is a usually a painless procedure and may actually be fun because you will get to play a groom before you actually become a groom.

First, you'll probably meet with the person who will be performing the wedding. They will then explain your duties to you, which includes things like:

> ➢ You stand there.

> ➢ You give your bride a ring.

> ➢ You say "I do" and maybe a few other words.

> ➢ You smile a lot.

Nothing you can't handle; especially since, during the rehearsal, there's no real pressure on you. (It's kind of like how hitting a home run is a lot easier in batting practice than in a game.)

During rehearsal you may also do things like:

> ➢ Go over the music they will play. By "go over" the music, we mean shake your head and agree with whatever the music person and your bride-to-be say.

➤ Watch carefully and lovingly as your wife practices walking down the aisle.

➤ Look around and nod knowingly as your bride and other people position the members of the wedding party in their proper places.

➤ Hang out and exchange jokes with the ring bearer. (He'll probably be somewhere from five to eight years old, so you should get along just fine, but it'd be wise to avoid any jokes or limericks that start with: *There once was a farmer from Pawtucket*....)

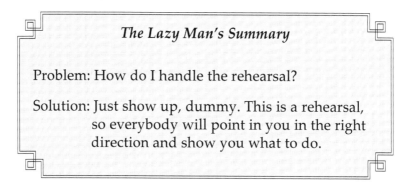

The Lazy Man's Summary

Problem: How do I handle the rehearsal?

Solution: Just show up, dummy. This is a rehearsal, so everybody will point in you in the right direction and show you what to do.

The rehearsal dinner

Rehearsal dinners are typically held the night before the wedding, immediately following the wedding rehearsal. This is for the friends and family who came to town for the wedding and/or are in the wedding party and is meant to be a time to unwind and enjoy.

Hopefully, it will be relaxing, but don't be surprised if something not so relaxing happens—after all, your family will be there and your family is weird. Plus, your fiancée's family will be there too and you'll quickly learn your family isn't the only weird one because while families may love each other, they don't always like each other, so there are bound to be clashes of tempers and temperaments. (For instance, Uncle Bob doesn't like Uncle Sal. Or maybe Uncle Bob likes Uncle Sal's wife, Aunt Sally, a little too much. Or maybe Uncle Bob likes Uncle Sal's daughter Suzie a bit too much....)

On the friend front, the rehearsal dinner is customarily the time when the unmarried bridal (and groom) party members start to pair up. Nothing makes a single girl more anxious than a wedding. And your single friends (being the dogs they are) will try to take advantage of this—which can get especially interesting if the bridal party has one especially hot member.

All in all, things could get ugly or interesting. It all depends on your point of view. Your best bet is to remember this is why we have rehearsal dinners so we can get these things in the open before the wedding. Just let it roll.

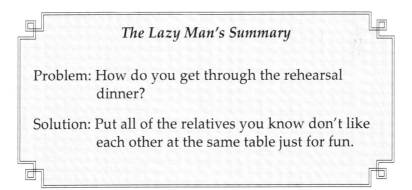

The Lazy Man's Summary

Problem: How do you get through the rehearsal dinner?

Solution: Put all of the relatives you know don't like each other at the same table just for fun.

The ceremony

This is what all the prepping, blood, sweat, tears and cash have been leading up to. After this, you will be man and wife. And this will probably be the easiest part. Yes, you may have a bit of stage fright, or even a bit of cold feet (see earlier section), but just take a few deep breaths and you'll be fine for your job is pretty straightforward. You mostly stand there.

Take for instance, how you'll be standing there when you watch your bride (the star) walk down the aisle toward you. This will be one of the proudest moments of your life. After all, this means somebody wants you! This moment will seem to unfold in slow motion.

Once your bride reaches you, the rest of the ceremony will fly by so fast you'll be shocked. You'll probably also be wondering, "What was all the fuss about?"

It's all going to be a blur. Just remember to keep breathing (inhale then exhale) and you'll be fine. But to summarize: Your role, in a nutshell, is to:

1. Nod your head and look attentive while whoever is performing the ceremony talks.

2. Take the ring from the best man and place it on your bride's ring finger. (Don't worry; she'll know which one it is.)

3. Say any vows you may have. (See section on vows.)

4. Say two words, "I do." (Or "I don't," in which case you should have stopped reading quite a while ago. Nevertheless, we thank you for your patronage.)

5. Kiss the bride. Then walk out of the building and get pelted with some sort of biodegradable material.

 *WARNING: For the night and the meal before the wedding, it's probably best to avoid foods like beans or cabbage or pretty much anything else that will give you gas or heartburn, for while you might find it entertaining to make the wedding party and the first couple rows of people pass out, your bride probably won't.*

The Lazy Man's Summary
(on how to get married)

The good way: "David, do you take Courtney to be your wedded wife, to live together in marriage? Do you promise to love her, comfort her, honor and keep her? For better or worse, for richer or poorer, in sickness and health? And forsaking all others, be faithful only to her? So long as you both shall live?

David takes a deep breath and says, "I do."

(cont.)

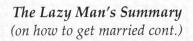

The Lazy Man's Summary
(on how to get married cont.)

The not-so-good way: "Melvin, do you take Shanice to be your wedded wife, to live together in marriage? Do you promise to love her, comfort her, honor and keep her? For better or worse, for richer or poorer, in sickness and health? And forsaking all others, be faithful only to her? So long as you both shall live?

Melvin takes a deep breath and thinks, *I know I really should have thought this through a little better*, then finally says, "I guess I do...."

The pictures

While the photographer will certainly take "action" pictures of the wedding ceremony, party and process, you will also find it necessary to pose for pictures. These pictures are obviously important because in the years to come they will give you something to look back on and say, "Boy, I used to be skinny and have more hair."

And if there are any lingering doubts in your mind that your bride is the star of the wedding, the posing for pictures will shatter those doubts, then stomp on them, then chew them up, spit them out, and then stomp on them again for your bride will pose for more pictures this day than Gisele Bundchen ever did in a year (except, of course, for any year Gisele married Tom Brady).

Now, yes, you will also pose for a lot of pictures (probably a lot more than you want), but your bride will be in more and always the center of attention. But, this is a good thing because your bride is a lot easier on the eyes and the camera lens. Sure, you got all dressed up and look nice, but brides get radiant when they put on a wedding dress. So, it's good to have a person around to document it with pictures.

As to the pictures themselves, there are many possible permutations:

 ➢ The bride alone from many angles, in many poses, in front of many different backgrounds. (2,314 shots)

 ➢ You alone. (4 shots; after all, there is only so much a camera can do….)

 ➢ The bride with you. (42 shots. Sure, there are only two of you, but she'll still be the focus.)

 ➢ The bride with her family. (29 shots)

 ➢ The bride with her extended family. (15 shots)

 ➢ The bride with your family. (1.5 shots)

 ➢ The bride and you with her family. (2 shots)

 ➢ The bride and you with your family. (2 shots)

 ➢ The bride with the bridesmaids. (At least 150 shots)

 ➢ The bride with the groomsmen. (7 shots)

 ➢ You with the groomsmen. (1 shot)

 ➢ You with the bridesmaids: if you are lucky. (1 shot, at very most)

 ➢ The bride with any ring bearers, flower girls, etc. (37 shots)

The entire picture-taking process will take anywhere from close to an hour to way, way more than an hour. Yet, no matter how long it actually takes, it will seem a lot longer to you and your guests, but at least your guests get to relax at the bar, munching on the thousands of dollars worth of *hors d'oeuvres* you had to work three weeks overtime to pay for.

Your only choice here is to grin (and grin, and grin) and bear it. Look at it this way, it will make your bride a happy woman. It also helps to keep repeating to yourself, "I look so good in the tux. I look so good in the tux…." That should make you feel better.

The honeymoon

This should be a very happy time, but if you need to read a book about what to do on your honeymoon, this isn't the book you should be reading. 'Nuff said.

Life-ever-after

Your first few days of being a married man are going to be different, but it will be a good different. The big trick is to remember you are married. It won't be hard, just different—after all, up until now you've spent all of your life not married.

The first time you introduce the lady next to you as *"my wife,"* it's going to be weird. But, once again, it's going to be a good kind of weird.

Yes, you may even have the urge to laugh a bit as the words come out of your mouth (for it may sound a bit funny to you), but however it sounds or feels, you should suppress the urge (for while it may be a good laugh for you, your "now wife" probably won't think of it that way....).

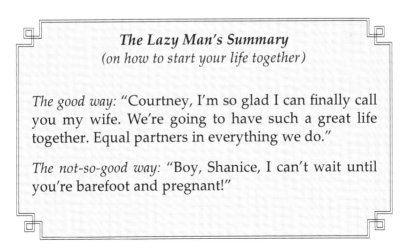

The Lazy Man's Summary
(on how to start your life together)

The good way: "Courtney, I'm so glad I can finally call you my wife. We're going to have such a great life together. Equal partners in everything we do."

The not-so-good way: "Boy, Shanice, I can't wait until you're barefoot and pregnant!"

Appendix

Wedding history and trivia

 Note: This info is gleaned from the web, so none of it could possibly be made up....

> The tradition of bridesmaids dressing the same as each other and in similar style to the bride comes from ancient days when it was believed evil spirits would have a more difficult time distinguishing which one was the bride and not be able to put a hex on her. Today, the hex is having to wear those God-ugly dresses.

> According to English folklore, Saturday, the most popular American choice, is the unluckiest day to marry. It would be interesting to compare the divorce rates between Brits and Americans married on Saturdays compared to those married on other days. (Okay, maybe it wouldn't be that interesting, but there's a good chance that some lonely social scientist has probably done it....)

> Queen Victoria made white the bridal color of choice when she wore it to wed Prince Albert in 1840. (The theory is she had stock in a company that specialized in white fabric.)

> ➤ The reason the engagement ring and wedding band is worn on the fourth finger of the left hand is because the ancient Egyptians thought the "vein of love" ran from this finger directly to the heart. Today, science has shown the "vein of love" is actually the throat and it is stimulated by large qualities of beer.

> ➤ The average wedding costs around $25,000 with 200 guests. Obviously, the more guests you have, the more it costs—you do the math.

> ➤ In Pennsylvania, ministers are forbidden from performing marriages when either the bride or groom is drunk. If this were true in Vegas, weddings there would drop an estimated ninety-nine percent.

> ➤ The veil dates back to ancient Rome, when it was flame yellow, always worn over the face, and called a *flammeum*. (Apparently, ancient Roman woman were quite homely.)

> ➤ The kiss at the end of the wedding ceremony dates back to the way olden days when the couple would actually make love for the first time under the eyes of half the village. (Today we have X-rated movies, camera phones, and the Internet instead.)

> ➤ The tradition of tying tin cans to the back of the newlyweds' vehicle started long ago with the belief that items tied to the back of the couple's carriage would produce noise to scare away evil spirits. (And mothers-in-law, we suspect.)

> ➤ Fifty percent of first marriages end in divorce. Sixty percent of second marriages end in divorce, which really shouldn't be all that surprising since a hundred percent of second marriages have at least one member who has been divorced at least once.

➤ In the rhyme "something old, something new, something borrowed, something blue," the word "blue" is symbolic of the blood of royalty, since both the bride and the groom were once considered to be "royal" on their wedding day. (The old part also comes from the royal family itself being that most of them are pretty darn old.)

➤ In times past, if a young man encountered a blind person, a pregnant woman, or a monk while on his way to propose to his intended bride, it was believed the marriage would be doomed if he continued because those images were thought to be bad omens. On the other hand, if he were to see a pigeon, wolf, or goat, he could expect extremely good fortune in the marriage. The moral of this story is to visit the zoo, not a monastery or a hospital, before you go to propose.

➤ June has been the most popular choice for weddings—for a long, long time. Not because of the great weather, but because during the 1400 and 1500s, May was the month in which each person had their "annual bath." Back in those times, most people were only able to bathe thoroughly once each year. Therefore, June became a good time to hold celebrations because it was one of the few times of the year everybody didn't stink. June is also named after the goddess Juno, who was the Roman counterpart to Hera, the goddess of the hearth and home, and patron of wives.

➤ Bad weather on the way to the wedding is believed by some to signify unhappiness in the marriage. Traditionally, it is believed cloudy skies and wind on the way to the wedding will result in a stormy marriage. However, snow on the way to the wedding is a sign of fertility and prosperity. So, by this theory, Eskimos should be very fertile and China should be a lot less crowded.

Official definitions of wedding

To give the book an air of sophistication, this has been included for you really smart types who need to know this kind of stuff. (This is also included for those of you who like to impress people with useless knowledge.)

wedding

Wed \ Wed \, v. t. [imp. Wedded; p. p. Wedded or Wed; p. pr. & vb. n. Wedding.] [OE. wedden, AS. weddian to covenant, promise, to wed, marry; akin to OFries. weddia to promise, D. wedden to wager, to bet, G. wetten, Icel. ve[eth]ja, Dan. vedde, Sw. v["a]dja to appeal, Goth. gawadj[=o]n to betroth. See Wed, n.]

1. To take for husband or for wife by a formal ceremony; to marry; to espouse.
    With this ring I thee wed. —Bk. of Com. Prayer.
    I saw thee first, and wedded thee. —Milton.

2. To join in marriage; to give in wedlock.
    And Adam, wedded to another Eve, Shall live with her. —Milton.

3. *Fig.:* To unite as if by the affections or the bond of marriage; to attach firmly or indissolubly.
    Thou art wedded to calamity. —Shak.
    Men are wedded to their lusts. —Tillotson.
    [Flowers] are wedded thus, like beauty to old age. — Cowper.

4. To take to one's self and support; to espouse. *[Obs.]*
    They positively and concernedly wedded his cause. — Clarendon.

Source: Webster's Revised Unabridged Dictionary, ©1996, 1998 MICRA, Inc.

wedding   n

> 1: the social event at which the ceremony of marriage is performed [*syn: wedding ceremony, nuptials*]
>
> 2: the act of marrying; the nuptial ceremony; "their marriage was conducted in the chapel" [*syn: marriage, marriage ceremony*]
>
> 3: a party of people at a wedding [*syn: wedding party*]

Source: WordNet ®1.6, ©1997 Princeton University

Handy wedding definitions

Alimony: Something you'll either have to pay (or receive) if the wedding doesn't work out. (Hopefully, you won't have to deal with it but the book needed a definition for the letter A.)

Bachelor party: *(See: Recipe for Trouble.)*

Best man: One of your closest friends who will stand by you during the wedding. Some of his job duties will include: holding the ring, paying any priest and/or organist (with your money), making sure you don't back down, making sure you stay presentable even if you barf, and giving an embarrassing toast.

Bouquet: A bunch of expensive flowers your wife is just going to toss to her friends for them to fight over. (Actually, that alone makes them worth the price. *See: Cat fight.)*

Bride: The star of the wedding and your wife-to-be.

Bridesmaids: The star's support staff, of which your ushers will be hoping at least some of them are hot.

Cat fight: If you get lucky, what you'll see when your bride throws her bouquet to her unmarried friends.

Cummerbund: Something you wear that sounds about as comfortable as it is.

Debt: What you will be in after the wedding, unless you can talk your in-laws into paying.

Eloping: Running off somewhere to get married in front of a couple of witnesses. It avoids a lot of hassles and expenses and really irks your mom and mother in-law.

Favors: No, not begging your wife for sex. Favors are small gifts and trinkets you give to people who attend your wedding so they will remember it.

Golf: Something you won't be playing as much of now.

Garter: A piece of cloth your wife wears around her thigh. In the olden days they were probably used to hold up nylon stockings, but today they are just used to give you something to toss to your unmarried friends.

Groom: You.

Honeymoon: Long ago, this was in theory the first time you and your wife would have sex. Now it's more likely the first time you have sex as man and wife.

Justice of the peace: A person who specializes in performing marriage ceremonies.

Maid of honor: The bride's version of a best man. (Your friends are going to hope she's hot.)

Matron of honor: A married maid of honor. (Your friends will be depressed if she's hot.)

Reception: The party after the wedding that gives your friends and relatives a chance to offer you advice and make fools of themselves.

Recipe for trouble: Your friends. Too much alcohol. Camera phone. And a stripper. 'Nuff said. (Refer to chapter on bachelor parties.)

Rehearsal: Usually held the day before the wedding so everybody knows what to do. Your job will basically be "to stand there" and nod. You can do that. Right?

Rehearsal dinner: A small dinner with family members and the wedding party usually held the night before the wedding (after the rehearsal) so your bride can correct any bad eating displays you might have before a lot of people see them at the reception.

Sex: Something you will be getting a lot of at first…and less and less of as the years go on.

Shower: A party where your wife and a bunch of her friends get together and shower togeth— Nah, just wanted to make sure you were still paying attention. The shower is nowhere near that exciting. It is a party a bunch of your wife's friends throw for her so they can shower her with gifts and advice. (Hope you're not invited.)

Ushers: A bunch of your friends who will escort people to their seats at the wedding ceremony. It's a token job that a fairly intelligent trained monkey could do, but you've gotta figure your buddies would be more fun to hang out with at your wedding than a trained monkey. (Trained monkeys are mean drunks; plus, they tend to throw things you really don't want to think about.)

Veil: The covering over the bride's face as she walks down the aisle. This custom probably originated in ancient times, before makeup was invented (this way even the especially ugly brides would have a shot at getting married before the grooms had a chance to run).

Wedding: The actual ceremony that will go by so fast you won't believe you—well, your bride—spent so much time planning it.

Wedding party: Not really a party, just your bride's friends who she asks to be in her wedding and a few of your friends who you rope into being in your bride's wedding.

X-chromosome: Your wife has two of these, you have one. Kind of makes sense in a biological sort of way.

YMCA: A dance they, hopefully, won't do at your wedding.

Zinfandel: A wine you might have at your wedding…and included in this book to give a Z definition.

Other resources

Wedding websites

There are a bunch of them and they change daily (if not hourly). Just go to any preferred search engine and type "weddings." Then point and click to your heart's content.

Wedding magazines

There are still way more of these than you, being a guy, would ever think there would be. And your bride will probably read as many of them as she can. Plus, there are lots and lots more magazines for brides than for grooms, which is okay because while she's reading those, you can probably read your *Sports Illustrated* swimsuit issues without her noticing.

About the Authors

John Zakour is a humor/sf/fantasy writer with a Master's degree in human behavior. He has written thousand of gags for comics, comedians, and TV shows. He also writes his own syndicated comic, *Working Daze,* for United Media, which appears in papers world-wide (well, the U.S., Scotland, Poland and Taiwan). He's been a regular contributor to several magazines and comic books and written seven humorous SF novels for DAW books, three YA books, three self-help books, and three books on HTML. John's first humorous SF mystery book, *The Plutonium Blonde* (DAW 2001), co-written with Larry Ganem, was named one of the top thirty SF books of 2001 by *The Chronicle of Science Fiction*, which called it "the funniest SF book of 2001." John lives in upstate NY with his wife, Olga, a professor at Cornell University and his son Jay.

Chuck Schading is managing editor for the *Finger Lakes Times* newspaper in Geneva, New York. He and his wife, Rachael, planned extensively for their 2003 wedding before deciding the whole thing was an awful lot of trouble. At a party more than a month after they eloped, the couple served "Ómini-franks in dinner jackets" in honor of their own little wiener—a not-so miniature Dachshund named Mr. Whiskers. The Schadings live in Geneva with their two boys, Owen and Samuel.

The Couple's Guide to Pregnancy & Beyond
He Says, She Says

By John Zakour & Shannon Duffy
with Joanne Hessney, M.D

For couples interested in making the most out of this team project, *The Couple's Guide to Pregnancy & Beyond: He Says, She Says* offers parents-to-be of all ages hip, gender-specific perspectives about a full range of issues and concerns that both men and women face when it comes to pregnancy.

Each informative chapter contains an introduction, a section written from "She to He," another written from "He to She," and concludes with a bit of "banter between the sexes" that is designed to address some of the most commonly asked questions.

Also featured throughout is the sage medical advice of Dr. Joanne Hessney who provides even more information about pregnancy from a clinical perspective.

Reviews:

"...just what the doctor ordered...(a book) that addresses the expectant dad in a format that he'll actually read. It's straight-talking, humorous and written in "guy talk", while being sensitive enough to address the expectant mom's concerns. A true he/she bonding opportunity! Two thumbs up!" — Dave E. David, M.D. Nationally recognized Board Certified Obstetrician and creator of the video "Making Womb For Baby." http://www.drdavedavid.com

"We love this fun and refreshing approach to calming pregnancy fears for moms *and* dads." — Ellie & Melissa, co-founders of the nation's #1 maternity concierge and consulting company and planning experts for WebMD, DisneyFamily, Baby Zone, and Pregnancy Magazine. http://www.thebabyplanners.com

"A must-read if you're expecting. Duffy and Zakour share the honest truth about those exciting nine months and beyond. Spiced with humor, their suggestions will truly help expectant parents understand each other and what's happening in baby's first apartment—the womb!" — Blythe Lipman, author of "Help! My Baby Came Without Instructions," host of the Baby and Toddler Instructions radio show, and expert with 25+ years of experience in the field. http://www.babyinstructions.com

"A practical, delightful book chock full of valuable guidance for the expecting couple and gives them an expert map to embark on life's greatest adventure." — Stevanne Auerbach, PhD., Dr Toy, Author, Smart Play Toys. http://www.drtoy.com

"A great approach to a very challenging subject, and a book every father-to-be should read. Having gone through the magic of having children twice, I would have appreciated this direct yet light hearted approach to preparing for the big day." — John McPherson, Author, "Ten Simple Rules for Being a Better Parent in a World Turned Upside Down." http://www.tensimplerules.net

The Couple's Guide to Pregnancy & Beyond
He Says, She Says

Look for it from your local or online book retailer
or visit us at http://www.blueleafpub.com

ISBN: 9780975509586

Printed in Great Britain
by Amazon

14245965R00061